Think Like a Stoic

The Ultimate Guide to Becoming a Stoic, Learning the Art of Living & Overcome the Fear of Failure - Stoicism 101 the Philosophers Guide to an Ancient Philosophy

Written By

Marcus Epictetus

© **Copyright 2020 Marcus Epictetus - All rights reserved.**

This document is geared towards providing exact and reliable information in regard to the topic and issue covered. The publication is sold with the idea that the publisher is not required to render accounting, officially permitted, or otherwise, qualified services. If advice is necessary, legal or professional, a practiced individual in the profession should be ordered.

From a Declaration of Principles which was accepted and approved equally by a Committee of the American Bar Association and a Committee of Publishers and Associations.

In no way is it legal to reproduce, duplicate, or transmit any part of this document in either electronic means or in printed format. Recording of this publication is strictly prohibited and any storage of this document is not allowed unless with written permission from the publisher. All rights reserved.

The information provided herein is stated to be truthful and consistent, in that any liability, in terms of inattention or otherwise, by any usage or abuse of any policies, processes, or directions contained within is the solitary and utter responsibility of the recipient reader. Under no circumstances will any legal responsibility or blame be held against the publisher for any reparation, damages, or monetary loss due to the information herein, either directly or indirectly.

Respective author(s) own all copyrights not held by the publisher.

The information herein is offered for informational purposes solely and is universal as so. The presentation of the information is without contract or any type of guarantee assurance.

The trademarks that are used are without any consent, and the publication of the trademark is without permission or backing by the trademark owner. All trademarks and brands within this book are for clarifying purposes only and are owned by the owners themselves, not affiliated with this document.

Table of Content

Introduction 2

Chapter 1: Understanding the Philosophy of Stoicism 6

Chapter 2: Stoicism in the 21st Century 22

Chapter 3 – Modern Day Stoic Practices 36

Chapter 4 – All the Way to Emotional Resiliency 50

Chapter 5 – Get Rid of Stress, Trauma, Fear & Anger 66

Chapter 6: Stoicism & Mindfulness 83

Chapter 7 – Turn Yourself into a Better Person 97

Conclusion 110

Introduction 116

Chapter 1: Full Day Stoic Routine 121

Chapter 2: The Best Stoicism Exercises 134

Chapter 3: Mastering Self-Control 148

Chapter 4: Be a Stoic in the Workplace 164

Chapter 5: Discover Peace in Between Yourself 182

Chapter 6: Become a Modern Stoic 200

Chapter 7: Find Real Happiness 218

Conclusion 236

The Stoic way of Life

The ultimate guide of Stoicism to make your everyday modern life Calm, Confident & Positive

Written By

Marcus Epictetus

Introduction

Do you find yourself often backing out from promises you made to yourself? These un-kept promises can be as little as missing the gym, putting your alarm on snooze, or the long-overdue laundry sitting on your chair to as big as procrastinating on the yearly goals. Do you feel like you cannot stick up for yourself? You want to say "no" at times but end up painfully agreeing to everything. Do you care too much about others' opinions of you?

If the answer is "yes" to any of these questions, then you are like one of the many troubled generations; emotionally weak. As hard as it may be to accept that, growth can only begin when you confess your lackings to yourself. If you really wish to turn a blind eye to all that may be wrong, let me assure you then that there will never be any room for growth.

No one is perfect, and it is completely alright to admit that. Remember, shame is deliberately staying stuck, not seeking an opportunity for growth.

There are aspects contributing to emotional weakness. They can be as natural as genetics to what environment you were exposed to and how you dealt with it. It even varies with age. Emotional resilience is empowering, and I can show you how to master it. Now to answer the question of "how," let me introduce you to a school of Hellenistic philosophy, Stoicism.

The wisdom of this ancient philosophy is eternal, and its significance is undeniable in the search for a peaceful and fulfilling life. The principle of "Stoicism" asserts that virtue (e.g., wisdom) is that pleasure and judgment are based on actions rather than words, and we cannot control and should not depend entirely on external events but on ourselves and our reactions. But it is a very basic, but not convenient, way of life at the very root of thinking. Take challenges in your life, and develop them into your asset, control what you can, and embrace what you cannot.

In fact, many of the great minds of history not only recognized it for what it actually was but they even practiced Stoicism: Walt Whitman, George Washington, Frederick the Great, Adam Smith, Eugène Delacroix, Immanuel Kant, Matthew Arnold, Thomas Jefferson, Ambrose Bierce, William Alexander Percy, Theodore Roosevelt, Ralph Waldo Emerson. Each of them reads the Stoics, learned, quoted, or admired them.

According to the famous modern-day scholar and essayist Nassim Nicholas, "A Stoic is someone who transforms pain into transformation, fear into prudence, desire into undertaking and mistakes into initiation."

About 304 BC, a trader named Zeno was shipwrecked on a trade mission. He had lost almost everything. Finding his way to Athens, the Megarian philosopher Stilpo and the Cynic philosopher Crates introduced him to philosophy, which changed his life, and he gave birth to Stoicism.

Stoicism allows us to embrace and get past whatever the tragic occurrences that arise in our lives. It is a true philosophy of healing. A Stoic never feels sorry for himself, nor does he cause his emotions to undermine his thinking ability.

Stoic ethics was focused on basic precepts that, even today, are still very powerful. Epictetus explained the meaning of deciding what depends on us and what does not: Our tendencies, our judgments, our dislikes, and our interests are what depend on us; in a nutshell, everything that is an operation of our mind. What do not rely on us are the money, body, awards, and high office positions meaning things that are not our minds' outputs.

When you do not worry about other people's opinions, you can waste less time and put that time to use focusing on your own self and goals. There is no point worrying if something does not depend on us. On the opposite, we need to resolve this grief, according to stoic logic. The entire stoic ethic is about the proper use of justification that, under all situations, we should allow us to be in command of our experiences.

There are three prominent stoic teachers after Zeno; the playwright and political counselor Seneca, the Roman Emperor Marcus Aurelius, and a slave Epictetus.

Seneca was a philosopher and also a self-proclaimed adherent of Stoicism. Of all ancient thinkers, one thing that really stood out from Seneca was that he was one of the most exciting and readable things. Much of that was attributed to the fact that in the medium of letters came his most notable works. We have two key tips for you to take with. Seneca wrote not only a collection of essays dealing with such realistic problems- adversity, mortality, and frustration, but also tranquility, leisure, and happiness. He also wrote about a variety of natural science topics-thunder and lightning, rivers, earthquakes, comets-and he created a considerable body of dramatic work.

Popular historians wrote that Marcus provided evidence of his learning not simply by language or comprehension of metaphysical doctrines but by his blameless nature and temperate way of life. He governed better than anyone else who was ever in any position of influence, in addition to having all the other virtues. Maybe the only text of its kind ever made is Marcus's Meditations. It is the personal views of the most influential man in the world counseling himself on how to make good on the obligations and roles and of his positions. It is the authoritative book on personal integrity, self-discipline, modesty, power, and self-actualization,

Epictetus was born trapped in slavery. His Enchiridion, which is described as a 'small textbook or a handbook', would be an ideal starting point for Epictetus. As it is filled with brief Stoic maxims and values, it is the ideal introduction to Epictetus. After formal teaching had ended for the day, Epictetus' discourses, found in Koine Greek, the ordinary contemporary version of the language, seem to document the interactions between Epictetus and his pupils. What we have in it is a series of personal but serious conversations in which Epictetus attempts to help his students carefully consider what a Stoic's intellectual life consists of and how to live it. He addresses a huge variety of subjects, from friendship to sickness, from anxiety to hunger, how tranquility can be gained and sustained, and why other people need not to be upset with one another.

This compelling and highly actionable book will show you how you can get on with life itself effectively. It is not very common that everything valuable and meaningful to us goes exactly the way we want it to, and that is life. You have to deal with it. Now it is your choice, you want to do that either feeling helpless or feeling empowered.

Though if you choose the latter, this book has been written for you. It will act as your mentor in achieving self-control, self-resilience, and calmness.

Continue reading this book if you simply wish to become the best possible version of yourself.

Chapter 1: Understanding the Philosophy of Stoicism

A brief definition of Stoicism would be that it is the philosophy of developing a logical and peaceful approach to one's life experiences and exposure concentrating on what lies in your control and putting aside what does not.

A prominent tutor of Stoicism became the secret diaries of one of Rome's greatest emperors, the intimate correspondence of one of Rome's finest playwrights and wisest power figures, the teachings of a former slave and exile. These remarkable records survive, against all odds, about two centuries later. They comprise some of the greatest insight in the world history and together form the basis of what is known as Stoicism, an ancient philosophy that was once one of the most prominent civic disciplines in the West, exercised in the pursuit of the Good Life by the strong and the weak, the wealthy and the oppressed alike.

The philosophical theory called Cynicism was created by Antisthenes, one of Socrates' pupils. He taught that virtue is the only good (living in harmony with our perfect disposition of unselfishness and reason; therefore righteousness, prudence, temperance, and power) and the opposite is only ill, and that we should therefore not be affected by any external thing. Therefore, his school determined that the most important thing a person should do is to prepare themselves very vigorously to be able to behave virtuously in all circumstances. This meant finding difficult conditions aggressively and being virtuous in them. The Cynics were deliberately behaving according to social standards, educating themselves, regardless of reputation, to do the right thing. We participated in askesis, or exercise, where they voluntarily exposed themselves to extreme physical environments in order to increase strength. Diogenes, the Dog, famously lived in an urn and possessed nothing but a cloak and a stick; they lived as moderately as they could, and trained sobriety. He used to own a cup, but when he realized he could use his hands to drink, he destroyed it.

A while down the road, a rich merchant, Zeno of Citium, was shipwrecked in Athens and ended up chasing the Cynic Crates. He practiced as a Cynic for a while. He took issue with their ignorance of physics and logic; however (they did not worry about anything but ethics) and thought that it was not mandatory though askesis was beneficial. Ultimately, however, he developed Stoicism, teaching similar ethics, but without askesis mandating, and also with the study of logic and physics.

Stoicism is either unknown or falsely interpreted, even for the most ardent seekers of knowledge. This vivid, action-oriented, and paradigm-shifting way of life has become slang for "emotionlessness" or the ordinary person. Provided that the mere mention of philosophy makes it most anxious or bored, "Stoic philosophy" on the surface sounds like the last thing someone would want to hear about, let alone in the course of everyday life desperately needs.

Stoicism is an instrument in the practice of perseverance, self-mastery, and knowledge in its proper place: something one uses to live a wonderful life, rather than an obscure area of intellectual inquiry. It would be difficult to find a term that dealt with greater oppression at the hands of the English language than 'Stoic.'

About 301 BC, Stoicism was a class of ancient philosophy founded by the Phoenician merchant Zeno of Citium in Athens. It was initially named Zenonism, but since Zeno and his disciples gathered in the Stoa Poikilê or Decorated Porch, it came to be known as Stoicism.

The Stoics gathered in public outdoors, on such porch, where everyone might listen to the conversation. You might argue that it was somehow a 'street ideology' for common citizens, not just aristocrats.

Stoicism was one of the most powerful and widely esteemed schools of thought from the outset and for nearly five centuries. It was one of the most prominent public disciplines in the West, exercised in search of the Good Life by the wealthy and the weak, the strong, and the suffering alike. But over the years, almost two millennia, the information that was once so important disappeared from view and was almost forgotten.

It was just after the 1970s that the influence of Stoicism rose again mainly because it was the intellectual inspiration for Cognitive Behavioral Therapy (CBT) and because of the theory penned by writers such as William Irvine and Ryan Holiday.

Hopefully, the historical background of Stoicism has been quite clear by now. Now let's discuss the core principles and virtues of Stoicism.

1.1 Virtues of Stoicism

In Stoic theory, there are four essential values. According to the pioneer of Stoicism, Marcus Aurelius, if we are to come across something better than truth, righteousness, bravery, and self-control, it must also be something remarkable. It was almost 20 years ago. Since then, humans have discovered a lot of things, cars, the Internet, treatments for diseases that were once a death sentence, but have we discovered anything better?

Have we found anything better than being courageous?

Have we found anything better than moderation and sobriety?

Have we found anything better than doing what is right?

Have we found anything better than truth and understanding?

No, we have not. It is doubtful that we will ever. All we encounter in life is a chance to relate to these four characteristics. So, let's talk about justice, courage, temperance, and wisdom:

- **Justice**

    The most widely admired value by the Stoics is doing the right thing. There is no other more significant Stoic virtue than justice, for all are influenced by it. Marcus Aurelius himself considered justice to be the root of all the other virtues. Throughout history, Stoics have pushed and promoted justice, always a huge personal risk, and with great bravery, in order to do great things and protect the people and ideas they cherished.

    There are numerous activists and leaders who have taken to Stoicism to gird them against the challenge of struggling for the values that counted, to lead them in a world of so much wrong to what was right. A Stoic wants to assume profoundly that a person can make a difference. Effective advocacy and political maneuvering need awareness and planning, as well as realism and optimism. Wisdom, recognition, and also a refusal to recognize the status quo are necessary.

- **Courage**

    Seneca would say that he genuinely pitied people who had never suffered tragedy before. He said that no one would truly know what you are made of and capable of, not even you. You have gone through life without an enemy.

The universe needs to decide what group to put you in, which is why it will sometimes send you to your way complicated circumstances. Think about them not as inconveniences or tragedies, rather as options, as responses to concerns. Am I courageous? Am I going to face, or run away from, this problem? Am I going to stand up or get turned over?

Let your acts respond to the record and let them reassure you that the most important thing is courage.

- **Temperance**

Life is not, of course, so plain as to suggest that bravery is all that matters. While all will admit that bravery is necessary, we are all well aware of individuals whose bravery transforms into recklessness, and when they begin to risk themselves and others, it becomes a fault.

It is here where Aristotle comes in. In his famous "Golden Mean" metaphor, Aristotle simply used bravery as the main example. He said that there was cowardice at one end of the continuum, which is a lack of courage. There was recklessness, on the other hand, so much bravery. What was asked for was a golden mean. What we needed then was the proper quantity.

Temperance or moderation is about doing nothing in abundance. It is all about doing what is right in the right amount in the correct way. Since we are, in fact, what we repeatedly do, excellence is, therefore, a habit, not an act.

Virtue and quality is a way of life, in other words. It's basic. It's like an operating system, and habit is the code that this system runs on.

As Epictetus would later conclude that power is proven and develops in its subsequent actions, walking by walking, and, moreover, running by running. So, if you want to do anything, make a habit of it. So, if we want to be successful, if we want to excel, if we want to be amazing, we need to develop the skill we need to develop the everyday habits that allow this to happen.

This is terrific news. And it suggests that, without herculean initiative or mystical recipes, remarkable effects or enormous improvements are possible. Small changes, good processes, the proper procedures-these are the things that it takes.

- **Wisdom**

Temperance. Righteousness. These are life's critical values. What circumstances, therefore, call for courage? What is the amount that is right? What is the thing that's right? This is where it comes to the last and necessary virtue: wisdom, awareness, and learning; the experience needed for the environment to be navigated.

The Stoics have long valued wisdom. Zeno said that one mouth and two ears were given to us for a reason: to listen more than to talk. And because we have two eyes, we have a responsibility to learn and observe rather than we say.

In the modern days, just as it was in the ancient world, it is important to be able to differentiate between the massive clusters of information at your disposal and the true wisdom you need to live a decent life. It is vital that we learn that we keep our minds open forever. Epictetus said that you could not understand what you believed you already knew. That is real.

This is why we not only have to be humble scholars, but we also need to strive for great teachers. That is why we should be reading at all times. That is why we should not avoid practicing. That is why we have to be vigilant in filtering the signal out of the chaos.

The aim is not only to collect knowledge but the right kind of knowledge. These are the teachings contained in Meditations, from the real Epictetus to the entrance of James Stockdale into the realm of Epictetus. These are the main details you need to absorb, breaking up from the background noise.

The universe has thousands of years of burning wisdom at its hands. You are likely to have the power at your side to discover everything you desire. So today, by calming down, being intentional, and seeking the wisdom you need, respect the Stoic virtue of wisdom.

These four virtues are fundamental to Stoicism.

1.2 Core Beliefs of Stoicism

There are many principles of Stoicism. To get a better understanding of the essence of Stoicism, let's move on to the core principles it dictates:

- **Agreement with Nature**

    The essential purpose of life was decided to be Eudemonia by all ancient schools of philosophy.

    Eudemonia, this life objective, is a little difficult to interpret. Think of it as human beings' ultimate happiness or satisfaction attainable—a lofty, flourishing, and smoothly flowing life: The Good Life.

To advance to the Good Life, the Stoics came up with several realistic tactics.

A human being is a logical animal. That is what distinguishes humans from sheep and beasts. We are unique, both for better and worse, from all the other animals on planet Earth. The point of concern is not that we have different skin, smaller teeth, or thinner bones, but our social and mental skills.

Our potential for reasoning is what differentiates humans from all other animals. Since doing so negates our dignity, the most valuable and natural thing we have, we do not live like sheep or beasts.

Living in harmony with nature is about behaving like a human being rationally instead of like a beast arbitrarily (and out of passion). In other words, in all our acts, we can still apply our innate capacity to 'reason'. If we use logic, we live in peace with nature, so we behave as people are expected to behave. Humans are supposed to use rationality to act as humans, not as animals.

- **Focusing on the Control-able**

Allow the full use of what is in your control and, when it happens, take the rest. Some things depend on us, and some things do not depend on us. Epictetus just mentioned this philosophy at the beginning of his writing, Enchiridion. This idea is central to the stoic philosophy and doctrines of Epictetus. The most distinctive theory of Stoicism is essentially this so-called 'Stoic dichotomy of control.'

We have to differentiate carefully between what 'is up to us,' or under our own control, and what is not. Our voluntary decisions, including our acts and judgments, are up to us, while everything else is not within our influence.

For example, our bodies are not up to us, or at least not entirely. I think there are many things I can do to have a safe and desirable body. But this is only to a certain degree feasible. I can control my behavior and eat a balanced, high-fat diet, systematically workout and walk a lot, but I have little control over other aspects, such as my genes, my early exposure and interactions, and other environmental causes, such as diseases and accidents.

I monitor only my own actions, and I have to acknowledge with equanimity the result. By truly knowing that I am doing my best and doing everything in my power to get where I want to be, I get my happiness and trust. So, either I can accept the outcome easily because I know I did my best, or I cannot because I know secretly that I did not do my best.

This is a huge morale builder in my mind. To fulfill your tasks, you do everything you can and everything that is beyond your control. And then you happily head through the moment of reality, when you have done your very best. If the result is not satisfactory, you will simply embrace it and say, 'Well, I did my very best.'

You can reflect on what you can control and acknowledge what you cannot. You know that you have not done your best, or you have not acted appropriately when you feel the need to justify yourself.

The most important things about life are the things that are up to you, your emotions, and your actions. The most attractive part of Stoicism is that we are responsible for our growth because we are responsible for all that really matters in life. So, the biggest thing to take away here is to direct our energy and where we have the most strength and then allow the world to take care of the rest.

- **Living by Virtue**

What the Stoics meant by 'virtue' in terms of our logical human existence was excellent or thriving. Basically, you are enjoying the Good Life because you live according to virtue. In various types of virtue, this individual perfection takes place, or, simply put, we will excel in various ways. The Stoics listed these numerous types of virtues as the four cardinal virtues that we have discussed above.

Today, as you live according to these values, you are moving towards the true purpose of creation, the Good Life, or Eudemonia. So, the perfection of purpose and behaving according to virtue, or being 'virtuous,' is the secret to behaving the Good Life.

And if you uphold all the virtues, would you be noble in the Stoic sense. For starters, if you behave bravely during the day and then get drunk at night, you are not genuinely noble (because with all the binge drinking, you violate the virtue of self-discipline). Virtue is a kit for all-or-nothing.

It was obvious to the Stoics that virtue would be a reward of its own. You do something, you do because that's the right thing to do. For your own sake, you behave in harmony with God, with reason, and according to the cardinal virtues. It does not matter what you get out of it because as you move into the Good Life, doing according to righteousness is satisfying in itself.

Again, the word 'virtue' really refers to excelling with one's own personality and applying reason in a safe and praiseworthy way.

- **Good vs. Bad vs. Indifferent**

The Stoics distinguished between things that were 'good',' evil' and 'indifferent'.

Justice, wisdom, bravery, and self-discipline are the cardinal virtues of good things. The inverse to these virtues is the negative ones, including the four vices to cruelty, folly, indulgence, and cowardice.

All the rest, but mostly life and death, glory and bad reputation, riches and hardship, enjoyment and suffering, and health and illness, are indifferent things. Indifferent things like fitness, wealth, and prestige can be summed up.

In short: The Good Life is absolutely oblivious to oblivious things such as fitness, prosperity, and prestige. Simply, they do not exist. They are neutral. If you are wealthy or poor, good or ill, the overall happiness does not matter. We should then learn to be 'indifferent to indifferent things' and learn to be content with everything nature puts on our plates.

Indifference does not imply coldness. On the opposite, because indifferent objects are not up to us, someone greater than us desires them, and we get to love them equally.

Although indifferent objects may not be 'good' in fact, some are nevertheless more desirable and superior to others. Therefore, the Stoics classified indifferent things from 'preferred' and 'dis-preferred.'

A rather rational view was taken by the Stoics. Indifferent beneficial things such as good health, fellowship, money, and good looks were listed as favored indifferents, while dispreferred were their opposites.

The Stoics, however, made harmonious, eudemonic life an attainable objective for all, regardless of social class, fitness, education, or appearance. While all of these virtues are preferred, they are also insensitive to leading a virtuous existence and are not necessary.

People will always choose pleasure over suffering, prosperity over hardship, and good health over illness, so go ahead and look for those things, but your dignity and living in harmony with virtue is not threatened by doing so. In other words, it is easier to suffer sorrows, poverty, or illness in a noble way than to achieve pleasure, riches, or health in a shameful one.

- **Taking Action**

Even though the Stoics regarded external things as indifferent, their own actions were not at all indifferent to them. They had to try to do the 'right thing,' and the Stoics had to behave in harmony with morality to get to the eudemonic world. The Stoics were the doers.

Stoicism is a very practical philosophy of living. It is not enough for the Stoics to learn about how to live a life of their own, but to really go out into the world and practice their ideas. By doing the right actions, you would earn the Good Life.

You should not be content with studying abstract thoughts on how to live your life, but you must apply those thoughts aggressively. Knowledge and information, if not implemented, are cheap and worthless.

- **Reverse Clause**

As Stoic learners, we are supposed to do the right thing and do our hardest to get there, but with equanimity, we are also supposed to embrace the result. Do the very utmost to excel and realize and understand equally that the end consequence is beyond the direct control. We develop a strategy and do everything to fulfill our objective, but we realize at the same time that something can happen and deter us from completing our objective. We accept that and change our approach to the new situation, and aim to do the best we can again.

As starters, in sports, you concentrate on the process, you concentrate on the commitment, the planning, the training, and everything in your control, and you take the outcomes as they come. Being the best player and doing the best you can, is the main objective, not the winning.

- **Practicing Misfortune**

The concept of adversity premeditation is to envision potentially "evil" situations repeatedly beforehand so that they do not take you by surprise, and you will be able to face them peacefully and behave according to virtue.

No matter how disastrous a scenario might seem, those external circumstances are neither good nor evil for the Stoics, nor indifferent. It is just our responses that can be positive or evil. So, get your mind prepared and introduce yourself by creativity to tough scenarios, and in real-life situations, you will be safer and less vulnerable.

- **Loving the Undesired**

The Stoics encourage us to genuinely enjoy what has happened, whatever it is, instead of merely embracing what happens. It is a bit unnatural to have a love for something that we never wanted to occur. Think about a higher force that turns the globe and rules on everything that happens. And all incidents happen directly to you, whether desired or unexpected. It can feel wrong at the moment when something happens, but it serves something bigger that you do not yet understand, which will eventually help and benefit you.

- **Making Opportunities**

It is all about how we understand what happens around us and what we determine what those events mean. How we understand the universe and how we perceive what is happening to us make a gigantic change in the way we live our lives. This makes your life accountable to you. External events are not controlled by you, but you control how you want to look at them and then react to them. And, that is all what counts, in the end. The secret to recognizing these possibilities lies in your interpretation. It is much more important how you see things than the things themselves. In all, you will see the positive. Stoicism encourages one to think of anything as a chance for progress. This encourages one to turn everything, challenges and gifts alike, into opportunistic causes.

- **Mindfulness**

Mindfulness is a requirement for the practice of Stoicism, but it is often strengthened further through practice. It functions in both directions. Again, being attentive is about being alert enough to take a step back from your own feelings and then being able to select the right action instead of working on autopilot.

When you witness an emotion, you need to know that you feel that emotion at the exact moment; only then you can determine whether or not the feeling is beneficial and what the best reaction is. If you do not realize that you are behaving out of emotion, choosing and modifying your actions is incredibly difficult.

These ten core principles of Stoicism encompass the roots and basics of this school of thought. Let me introduce you to some famous philosophers of Stoicism in the next section.

1.3 Philosophers of Stoicism

Stoicism can do wonders for mankind. Without flinching, self-mastery and inner determination make it possible for Stoics to go through exceedingly adverse situations, all the time trying to behave rationally and logically. The keen understanding of the unpredictability of the universe and of the briefness of life is at the heart of Stoicism. Stoics, however, are not willing to spend time and resources on futile discussions or initiatives. The transition of negative thoughts into a sense of perspective prepares us to have the ideal state of mind at work and in our personal lives to make the right choices.

The ancient Stoic philosophers come from nearly every perspective imaginable. One was a slave, the other a king. One was a carrier of water. The other was a popular playwright. Some were traders. Others were independently affluent. Some of them were senators, and some of them were soldiers. The philosophy which they taught was what they all had in common. They concentrated not on the external world but on what was entirely in their own influence, whether they were leading the Roman army or chafing under the shackles of slavery: their own feelings, their own acts, their beliefs.

Marcus Aurelius served as the Roman Emperor for almost two decades. The gravity of that place and the degree of influence Marcus possessed is necessary to remember. At the moment, he occupied the world's most influential role. Nothing would be off-limits if he wanted to. There was nobody who could restrain him from all of his urges. He could indulge and submit to temptations. There is an explanation of why the saying that power has become a cliché throughout the history of absolute corrupt. And yet he proved himself worthy of the position he was in.

Seneca, who was born in southern Spain over 2000 years ago and was raised in Rome, is the second most influential Stoic in history. Seneca was an influence on prominent figures such as Francis Bacon, Pascal Erasmus, and Montaigne. For men and women in action, Seneca's Letters from a Stoic are a must read, providing timeless metaphysical wisdom on riches, sorrow, faith, strength, and life.

What makes researching Stoicism interesting is that in terms of where they stood in society, three of the most well-known practitioners varied extensively. One of the world's most powerful positions was occupied by Marcus Aurelius, the emperor of the Roman Empire. Seneca was an emperor's adviser, a famous playwright, and one of the Roman Empire's wealthiest citizens. And then there's Epictetus, on the other hand, who was born a slave. This is what makes Stoicism so powerful: it can have timeless virtues to assist us in both good and poor fortune, regardless of our position in life. For decades, his work inspired the masses and was even accepted as the central ideology by Emperor Marcus Aurelius.

This chapter covers the essential fundamentals of Stoicism, and in the next chapter, we will discuss that Stoicism is not just an old philosophy, it is a contemporary philosophy and how you can apply Stoicism to the modern world.

Chapter 2: Stoicism in the 21st Century

Stoicism is a way of life, not just some ancient theory restricted to dusty philosophy books. You cannot get away from it. It would even remain applicable in the hundred years to come because it speaks to our feelings and emotions, which are the true essence of the human soul.

Now I will guide you through the journey of Stoicism in a nutshell before we move onto its relevance to the modern-day world.

2.1 Journey of Stoicism

The ultimate purpose of our lives is eudemonia for stoics: a state of prosperity and contentment that can be accomplished by living in line with nature. Existing with nature involves both serving your purpose in the world and existing as a human being (which is very closely linked to conceptions of destiny and providence). Since human beings, through their capacity to use reason, separate themselves in essence of their existence from all living beings, they should behave according to their justification. We have to behave rationally, in short, and not allow our emotions fool us. There are neither positive nor negative external conditions, but it is better that we are oblivious to them. Over thousands of years, this purpose of eudaimonia i.e. contentment and growth and the methods of reaching it have been established.

Let's have a brief description of the golden age of Stoicism. It is the period, which starts from 300 BC and ends in 200 AD. This golden period is typically split into three parts: the early, the middle, and the late stoa. The last one is better known, as only sources still present are from that time. Let's get into it:

- **300 BC – 100 BC**

About 300 BC in Athens, Zeno of Citium founded the school of thought Stoicism. He rejected the famous school of thought Epicurism, put forward by Epicurus, who, motivated by pain and pleasure, inclined towards a materialistic universe and an unintended existence. From (among others) the teachings of Cynicism, which prioritizes simplicity and virtue, Zeno established his school of Stoicism. At the Stoa Poikile in the middle of Athens, he began teaching. It was covered, freely available colonnade that produced the name of his school of thought: Stoicism. The cornerstone of Stoicism was laid by Zeno, and the school had an immense influence. In three areas: logic, physics, and ethics, he developed a distinction in stoic philosophy. Most focus is on ethics now, even though the founder Zeno would argue the idea that logic and physics must support ethics.

Zeno was replaced by Cleanthes, his pupil, who largely adopted Zeno's teachings and incorporated a bit of his own. Chrysippus of Soli was the third chief (scholar) of the school stoicism. The three pieces of philosophy were greatly developed by him, most known by creating a framework of propositional logic. Chrysippus maintained the status of Stoicism as one of the greatest philosophies of all time by extending and solidifying the groundwork laid by Zeno. After him, Diogenes of Babylon, Zeno of Tarsus, and Antipater of Tarsus led the academy.

- **100 BC- 1 AD.**

The prominence of Stoicism began to move to Rhodes and Rome from Athens, beginning about 100 BC. The seventh scholar, Panaetius, was a lot more pragmatic than the stern Zeno in his views. He found stoic theories about physics easier and was a lot less concerned with logic. This moved the philosophy of Stoicism closer and more accessible to Neo-Platonism. He introduced Rome to Stoicism as well.

Panaetius is known to be the last scholar, owing to the more extensive and diverse existence of the middle stoa, accompanied by variations of opinion. A united and undisputed philosophy of Stoicism was no longer available, but stoic school of thought would prove to be able to survive the challenging test of time.

Posidonius re-ensured Panaetius' theories and got even closer to Aristotle and Plato. In Rome, Stoicism was embraced by Cato The Younger and Cicero. It is particularly possible to view Cato, famous for his inflexible moral honesty and his strict way of life, as a sign of Stoicism. He appears more closely identified with Chrysippus and Zeno's traditionalist doctrines than with Posidonius and Panaetius' diverse philosophy.

- **1 AD – 200 AD**

The main field of concern for stoic philosophers in the Roman Imperial era was ethics. Physics and logic have not been investigated as much anymore. Two hundred years long late stoa, since it is the sole time period from which full original writings are still in existence, is the best-known time of Stoicism. One of these texts comes from Seneca, who, in his Moral Letters to Lucilius, used real day-to-day events to address moral problems. He is highly admired for his own writing style, and he still reads his Epistulae today. For his Discourses and Enchiridion, which were issued by his student Arrian, another stoic philosopher, Epictetus, is known. The Handbook of Epictetus is a decent start if you are searching for an introduction to Stoicism. Though Epictetus was born into slavery, Marcus Aurelius emperor of Rome was probably the most famous Stoic. Ta eis heauton, which he initially wrote as a private diary during his military operations in Germany, is his most influential work. That is now widely referred to as Meditation. "Meditations" is perhaps the stoic work that is most debated and read and still provides inspiration for a better life to people today around the world. In our contemporary age, notions like reason, self-discipline, age, and citizenship are still important concepts. Meditations by Aurelius are still seen as a means of personal growth and development and have aroused renewed attention in recent years.

These were the three prominent periods of the growth of Stoicism. Now let's understand how Stoicism can still be practiced in the modern era.

2.2 Modern Day Stoicism

Stoicism has been around for an extensive period of time, and for quite a while, its penetration into Western thought has been happening. The stoic theory has inspired poets, theorists, and politicians over the centuries and indirectly weaved it into many Western thinkers' works.

There are many Facebook groups on Stoicism. The biggest of which has more than 25 000 participants as of 2017, and the Stoicism Subreddit (2017) has over 54,000 subscribers. There are email lists on which fierce disputes rage over points of theoretical detail: various Stoic blogs, some Stoic advisors, and hundreds of videos on YouTube.

There is a "Traditional Stoicism" website that has broken away from the other "new" communities on the basis of an insistence that devotion to ancient Stoic physics and theology is needed to live according to Stoic ethics.

There are the "Modern Stoicism" and "How to be a Stoic" email feeds, in which posts are written every single day on Stoic facts, texts, and topics, and, in the latter case, a common Stoic Advice column.

In comparison to, or as a corollary to, Stoic beliefs, some organizations propose Eastern meditative beliefs to "mindfulness."

Then there is a website "Daily Stoic" that sends email addresses to subscribers' daily Stoic meditation themes: whether quotations from the great Hellenistic and Roman Stoics or from literary and metaphysical works on Stoic themes. For many causes, Stoicism, though, has made a surprising apparent re-emergence:

- **Socialization Structures Failure**

There were structures in several years past that could be counted on by an individual to help him make sense of life. The church, the classrooms, and the family unit were some of these. Many of these systems have been significantly weakened in our current society and/or are no longer as important.

Many individuals do not really go to church, schools cannot compete with the Internet, and single parents are the heads of many households.

You have a future where the next day is different from the previous, leading to the fact that the digital world produces tidal landscapes of transition. People are looking to the perennial essence of secular Stoicism for guidance to find a grounding in this turbulent universe.

- **Massive Accessible Information**

In just one week, more information is produced than was produced in the first several thousand years of human existence. Ideas circle across the globe so quickly that one can catch on and grow viral extremely rapidly.

Stoicism speaks to the people because everybody wants to improve himself. They just want to be stronger. Everyone wants more sense of self. People want their lives to be more in their control. On all of these, Stoicism provides a simple prescription. You can add that to the fact that every year there are many fantastic books and websites on Stoicism and modern Stoicism published and launched. You have the easy accessibility to the contents of ancient philosophy with several loads of them.

- **Undeniable Advice**

In all times, stoic wisdom extends to everyone everywhere. This is the concept of a "perennial philosophy." Human nature, no matter what tradition or place of origin it comes from, will still be human nature. In addition to witnessing the vastness that life has to offer, Stoicism at its heart reflects on how to cope with human existence (other people's and your own). It is very enticing.

The significance relies on a few very basic assumptions and concepts that are powerfully intuitive.

These begin with the clear call of Epictetus to individuals to always differentiate between what is not and what is in our power. There is no logical argument, at any fundamental stage, of being disappointed with the things we cannot change. To reflect on what we can influence, learning to let go of these things, our own current desires, emotions, and acts, just need to be both philosophically astute and a therapeutic boon.

Imagine that all people with mental energy invest thinking about what others think about them, tweet about them, do not like, or say or do not say about them. What may happen in the future or maybe even not, and what cannot be changed in the past, would be freed up to attend only to the things that can be changed at present.

This way of thinking will get you close to what the Stoics pledge, through their (Socratic) emphasis that the inner character (virtue) of individuals is the most valuable thing that anyone may reward or seek,

All of the other external aspects are "indifferent" to the Stoics, from prestige to fame to influence wealth to anything open to the adverse factors of outrageous fortune.

That is, they are neither good nor evil in themselves, nor does their possession or loss "make us" happy or sad. It is our opinions of objects that confer this influence over us upon them. Except by argument, certain decisions may be contested and reframed by experience and determination.

Stoicism has recently been reported as one of the best "mind hacks" ever invented, in today's words. Despite the destruction of their towns, houses, and loss of acquaintances or even loved ones, the resultant advertised capacity of Stoic "sages" to be able to hold up "philosophically" has earned the school the perennial image of being joyless, "grin and bear it" affair.

However, in order to achieve inner harmony, the Stoics do not wish or require individuals to sacrifice anything. Instead, Stoicism asks citizens to cultivate internal capital in order to be equanimity able to cope with success and hardship.

Stoicism has remained one of the permanent threads out of which Western culture has been woven, from the Serenity Prayer to Roosevelt to Shakespeare to contemporary writers such as Tom Wolfe or Walt Whitman.

And while most of us can find certain features of international Stoic physics and theology, there appears to be nothing about this ethic that is or will ever be ancient. Until today's 21st century renaissance in the banner of Stoicism, this realization prompted the pioneers of Cognitive Behavioral Therapy to incorporate Stoic concepts and recommendations into 20th-century psychotherapy.

By reading the above-mentioned reasons and justifications, I am sure you have understood that Stoicism is very much relatable and applicable in the present. There are many famous modern time personalities who follow Stoicism, and some even preach it. Let me get you through them one by one briefly.

Revival of Stoicism

While the influence of Stoic teachings during the Middle Ages was primarily limited to solving problems of social and political importance, it persisted for the Renaissance to provide the foundations for the resurgence of Stoic views in epistemology, logic, and metaphysics, as well as the recording of the more common Stoic theory, in its zeal for the rediscovery of Roman and Greek antiquity. There are many philosophers who brought the light back to Stoicism like Justus Lipsius, Giordano Bruno, Pietro Pomponazzi, Huldrych Zwingli, Blaise Pascal, Benedict de Spinoza, etc.

I have jotted down below some personalities who followed Stoicism in their path to success, and I am sure you will be surprised by many of the names:

- **Bill Gates**

Bill Gates followed the message of staying humble if we want to learn and succeed. Epictetus is, of all the Stoics, the nearest to a real teacher. He had a classroom. He had classes hosted. In reality, through a student who has taken very good lecture notes, his wisdom is handed on to us. One of the aspects that irritated Epictetus about students of philosophy, and irritated all college professors throughout history, is how students pretend to want to be educated but really secretly assume they know it all already. In today's upcoming entrepreneurs, you see this regularly: arrogance mixed with a lack of modesty before the eventual collapse.

The truth is, most of them are guilty of believing that we know best, and if we put that mentality down, we would all understand more. There is always someone who is better, is more successful, improved, and wiser than we are, as clever or successful as we can be.

Ralph Waldo Emerson, the writer of the 19th century, put it well that any man he encounters is his master at some stage. In some of the most popular market executives, we occasionally see this style of mindset. They are humble and seek suggestions actively and learn from everyone they know. Sam Walton, Walmart's founder, suggested that we should learn from everyone.

You also see that in Bill Gates, Microsoft's co-founder and philanthropist, a voracious reader who every day wants to learn the world a little bit, one book at a time. It is a humbling reminder of just how little you know, even though you are one of the most famous business magnates in the history, to continually open yourself to new insights and ideas.

- **Elon Musk**

Elon Musk followed the message of nothing to make anything just out habit. An employee is asked, "Why did you do things this way?" The response is, "because it's the way we have always done things." This reaction frustrates any successful employer. The employee has stopped thinking and is working out of habit mindlessly. Any logical boss will ask the worker to leave.

Can you agree that this is the mindset of a hyper-successful entrepreneur like Elon Musk? Not, of course! As he said that it is the best piece of advice to think endlessly about how you can do it differently and challenge yourself.

To our own working practices, we should add the same ruthlessness. In reality, to crack the rote behavior, we should research philosophy specifically. Out of memory or habit, find what you do and ask yourself: is this really the right way to do it? Understand why you do what you do. Do it for the correct reasons.

- **Pete Carroll**

Pete Caroll follows the message of turning failures into opportunities. Seattle Seahawks coach, Pete Carroll, is legendarily positive and also an understudy of Stoicism. Throughout his career, his coaching methods are focused on finding the inner grit of himself and his players, and taking on the supposed negative things that have happened and turning them into positive things. Carroll took the Super Bowl XLIX loss and onslaught of abuse over his final decision costing the Seahawks the game and pressed on into a new year. This is what the Stoics are doing.

- **Warren Buffett**

Warren Buffet follows the message of living below means. Warren Buffett, who basically has a net worth of about $85 billion, lives in the same house he purchased for $31,500 in 1958. A lineman for the Baltimore Ravens, John Urschel makes millions but manages to live on $25,000 (2017) a year. Also, with a deal worth some $94 million, Spurs star of San Antonio, Kawhi Leonard, gets around in the same 1997 Chevy Tahoe, he had, since he was a teenager. It is not that they are poor. It's because the stuff that matters to them is cheap.

Buffett, Urschel, and Leonard did not end up this way by mere chance. Their way of life is the product of prioritizing. They cultivate interests that are obviously beyond their financial means and, as a consequence, any revenue will give them the freedom to do the things they care the most about. It just happens that, beyond any expectation, they became rich.

In the universe, this kind of insight is what they love the most, which means that they will enjoy their lives. And if the markets were to switch or their lives were cut short by an injury, that means they would still be pleased.

A strategy understood by many business leaders is to live below your means. Amazon was deliberately designed by Jeff Bezos with a culture of frugality. According to him, he believes just as other constraints do, frugality fuels creativity. Inventing your way out is one of the few ways to break out of a small cage.

Mark Cuban, a billionaire businessman, has also promoted the ruthless reduction of unnecessary spending: The more you stress payments, the tougher it is to concentrate on your goals. The better you will work, the greater your choices.

Many of the palace furnishings were famously sold by Marcus Aurelius to pay off his empire's debt. He did not need luxuries, and they weighed him and his people down.

The more things we seek, and the more we have to do to earn or protect those accomplishments, the less our lives are truly valued and the less secure we are.

Let's get onto some daily life practicality of Stoicism.

Modern World Problems – Ancient World Solutions

Stoicism is, at its core, a philosophy of minimizing your life's negative emotions and enhancing your joy and gratitude; it includes rituals of mindfulness and living based on value. Stoicism, both externally and internally, is a method to amplify the human experience. I have put together some modern daily Stoicism life practices for you to follow:

- **Happiness Triangle**

The happiness triangle has three main elements, as mentioned below:

Eudaimonia, the fundamental purpose of existence agreed to by all ancient philosophies, is at the center of the triangle. This is the greatest promise of Stoic philosophy, and it is about leading a supremely peaceful and smoothly flowing life. In our lives, it is about thriving. Essentially, that is what we all desire, to prosper and live happier lives, right? This is why it is at the center of the Triangle of Stoic Happiness. Do you recall the word's Greek origin? It means being with your inner daimon, your supreme self, on good terms (eu). And how can we accomplish that? Through living with Areté.

Each-moment, express your ultimate self. We need to seal the gap between what we are capable of and what we actually do if we want to be on great terms with our highest self. Actually, this is about being your best version of the here and now. It is about using reason and working in accordance with profound ideals in our behavior. Obviously, this is better said than achieved, and what helps this optimistic aim is to distinguish good from evil and rely on what we manage. Concentrate on What You Control: In Stoicism, this is the most influential theory. We ought to reflect on the items we manage at all times and take the rest as it arises. It is necessary to accept what is already because it is beyond our power to undo it. Ultimately, what is beyond our power is not essential for our flourishing. What is important for our wellbeing is what we want to do with the external conditions provided. So, it is always within our power, no matter the situation, to try to make the best of it, and to live with our ideal self in harmony.

Taking responsibility is the last element. Good and bad come exclusively from yourself. This continues the first two corners that say external factors do not matter for the good life, so it is enough to succeed in life to survive with areté, which is beyond your reach. Often, because of any external incident you do not control provides an environment you do control, including how you want to react to this incident; you are responsible for your life. In Stoicism, this is crucial; it is not events that make us happy or sad, but our understanding of such events. The day you choose to allow outside circumstances no more control over you, this is when a tower of strength will be born.

- **Avoiding Materialism**

It appears like our consumerist culture creates more appetite than it satisfies. Our relentless media and commercial consumption leave us wanting and finding better out there, wasting our hard-earned dollars on the new fad, being assured that it would leave us happy before next year's arrival of version 2.0. Our appetite reduces as we tend to want less, and we become more content with what we have.

- **Be Genuinely Content**

You may have realized by now that satisfaction comes from inside and from appreciating everything around us, including something as basic as living at the moment in time where we can buy bottled water from a vending machine no more than 200 feet from us for $1.00 (sometimes we really take it for granted). Because our satisfaction will become independent of other influences with the stoic mentality, we can be satisfied as stoics all the time, and we want nothing more than human experience. We could cause ourselves to be frustrated if we wished for more. This does not suggest that stoics do not appreciate the better things of life; it just implies that we do not think of them for our pleasure as well. It can only leave us completely content by bringing goodness to the world by supporting others and advancing humanity, which we can do on a daily basis.

- **Picture the "What If"**

    We have now learned that desire for having more leads to unhappiness, but how do we find happiness? In gratitude, the key lies. Everything that we have, we have to respect and take satisfaction in it. With convenient access to essentials and innovations, we live in an unprecedented time of history that offers a quality of life that was unforeseeable just a few decades earlier. We take this for granted instead of appreciating it. One of the stoic traditions is to consider sacrificing any of your prized belongings. It can initially sound depressing, but we come to understand what we have more by imagining these defeats. It is important that we do not put too much value on the things we have because they may not always be there. When you put emphasis on an external thing, and it is stripped away, the stoic may not be frustrated but more thankful that they have the thing, to begin with. Becoming a Stoic involves seeking satisfaction in everything you have. Anything from the cosmos is borrowed. Materials come and go, but there remains goodness, and joy lies therein.

These are some of the basic stoic practices you can incorporate in your life to make yourself more in control of who you are and stay content. Thus happy.

Chapter 3 – Modern Day Stoic Practices

We all realize deep down that there is something that we can do and be. Indeed, much guilt comes from recognizing that a certain situation could have been dealt differently than we did. We freak out over the minimal on our children and then torture ourselves for days after with shame over it. We have a project deadline due at school, and we procrastinate on it before we have no choice but to pull an all-nighter, the whole time we get it done, feeling nothing but pressure. None of this is new; for practically thousands of years, humans have been putting off things they have to do, obsessing about things beyond their grasp, and giving in to counterproductive emotions.

All of us even seem to get more reflective at the beginning of the year. We begin to reflect on how the year ended, where we are now, and how much we have improved or not. We dwell on what should have been done differently, how we have treated people, and what we have left undone. We make resolutions based on these reflections. We resolve that we are going to stop smoking or start working out, starting next year. The new year begins, and soon, sadly, we give in and return to our old ways at the first sign of trouble. We light the cigarette, we lash out at our wives, and we continue to suffer the bad feelings associated with ourselves being frustrated.

This is not to say that it is trivial to uphold all of these measures, but it does not alter the fact that it has to be achieved. The argument is that the practice of self-improvement is continuous, and the possibility for practice is everywhere. And it is not worth losing these chances. Here are a few Stoic practices that, no matter where you come from or what the conditions are, will support you all in every facet of your lives:

- **Stoic Acceptance**

Stoic acceptance is about recognizing what is beyond one's influence instead of what is. Human brains are vulnerable to agonizing about the past or the future. We will waste hours ruminating about incidents that are entirely fictitious. We need to establish an internal locus of control. Any of what exists in life is not within our influence. This undeniable reality was known by the Stoics, and so they concentrated on what they could do.

Born a slave, it would appear like there was no justification for Epictetus to think that he could control everything. He was severely crippled by a fractured leg his master had given him. Epictetus survived all hardships with grace.

Epictetus would argue that his thoughts, interests, and aversions still remained his, even though his property and even his body were not under his power. That was something he was in control of.

Nowadays, it is easy to get irritated. We are so used to comforts and amenities that even the smallest inconvenience triggers indignation within us. The normal instinct is frustration, if not anger, if the internet takes a moment longer than it should or if traffic stops for a minute.

It is not any of these breakdowns that make us dissatisfied. The dissatisfaction stems from the emotional response that we have chosen. The responsibility is on ourselves to ensure that our inner state of mind is not affected by the external events. Once we internalize that, it becomes clear that, regardless of our conditions, we have the power to be happy.

It is all about self-acceptance and self-honor. You have to tame your mind.

The worst betrayal a person can do to himself is to make his mind feel that he has lost his composure. And the only thing that you can do about yourself is to behave like a survivor while you can be a fighter. Do not be dominated by your emotions. Let your inner strength empower you to be fully alive.

If you are not a part of this game, then it might be tough for you to cope with the harsh realities of life. People are going to intervene, challenge your choices; they are going to flood you with all sorts of views. Maybe they will also convince you to become just like them. Do not just fall into that trap. Stay raw; stay true, because that makes you who you are.

We are not part of a competition, nor are we doing a marathon because we have got to keep an eye on the winning trophy. Keep yourself cool. Do not let the rat-race mess with your happiness.

You will understand that nothing is more crucial than your mental health once you lose your calm. Take time if you need some time to bounce back to life; take sufficient time to know which direction to go.

Not everyone has the same collection of goals, dislikes, or likes. So instead of hating the work or finding yourself in a certain place trapped. Making the best of what you do and making it your goal.

Just make peace with your mind, for not every person has the same life view. Therefore, to some, what luxury is for you can be ludicrous. Similarly, it might not be someone else's cup of tea to find satisfaction in the easiest stuff. You need to know that and respect the decisions of others.

Do not ask others to like what you like, as they will begin to dislike you. Instead of seeking to influence others, they only cherish their individuality.

We, humans, are beings that are complicated. But the truth is, there are people like us who think like us and have stories to share in the same way.

If you desire to sit alone and enjoy it, so it is completely fine. If you find happiness in solitude and 20 people like to be in a group, then chase solitude. Do not drive yourself in a certain direction just because others want you to do it. It will generate total confusion, and you might end up hating everything.

- **Time Misers**

All the intellectuals of history, according to Seneca, could never truly articulate their perplexity in the corruptness of the human mind. The slightest disagreement with a neighbor will mean hell to pay or even a foot of their estate, no person can give up, and but we quickly let others enter our lives. Worse than that we happily pave the way for others who would later command our lives. No one hands his money out to passersby. In opposition to that how many of us have handed out our lives to others! With money and property, we are tight-fisted, but think so little about wasting time. It is the one thing that we should all be the toughest guardians of.

There will be countless interruptions every day: calls, guests, emails, and unforeseen incidents. Booker Washington noted that the people who are willing to consume one's time with no reason are almost innumerable. On the contrary, a philosopher understands that these violations hamper us from doing the contemplation and work that we were supposed to do as our purpose on earth. This is why they defend their feelings and personal space so diligently against trespassers and vulnerable neighbors. They understand that more than any conference or article, a few minutes of reflection are more worthy. They also realize how meager time we are currently given in life and it is very easily possible to deplete our stocks.

It was the death of a friend who made businessman and entrepreneur Tim Ferriss realize that it is surprising that we waste time concentrating on the insignificant individuals who add little but their selfishness. We have to stop this and instead concentrate and abolish distractions, one of the best business minds from the last century, as Peter Drucker, put it that push yourself to set goals. If you cherish the thought that you have got time for everything, you are going to end up doing loads of affairs you do not have to do indulge yourself in.

We are reminded by the Stoic teacher Seneca that we may be good at defending our physical property, but we are far laxer at upholding our mental limits. It is possible to reclaim property; some of it still untouched by man. Time, however? Time is the most irreplaceable resource; instead of attempting to make the most of it, we should actually avoid spending too much of it so easily.

- **Defeating Fear**

There are many ways to negotiate and mitigate the effects of anxiety, but Stoicism provides one of the clearest ways to deal with your fear by trying to push through what you fear most-an essential heuristic for life where it is even more dangerous to postpone decisions out of fear of failure than to make a risky decision.

The ancient stoics continually reminded themselves and their followers that all of us are mortal and have only a short time to have an impact on the world.

Instead of denying, facing the fear of death head-on and accepting, it allowed the Stoics to be braver and more productive in their daily lives.

Seneca wrote that, as if we were coming to the very end of life, we must prepare our minds. Do not let us postpone anything. Every day, let us balance life's books. There is never a short time for those who put the final touches on their lives every day.

You will be more efficient and never run out of time to achieve your goals and tasks by having to confront the fear of death, Seneca suggests. Seneca writes for people who fail to encounter their fears that life is very short. If you continually put off action out of anxiety and fear, you cannot accomplish your objectives. Challenging your fears is the first step to achieving the goals you set.

In contemplating death and confronting their worst fears, ancient philosophers are not the first ones who have found value. CEOs such as Steve Jobs and Jeff Bezos are also taking a stoic approach to putting their fears in the light of personal or business mortality.

Steve Jobs gave a starting speech at Stanford in 2005 in which he addressed how focusing on his own mortality enabled him to conquer his fears of failure. Jobs said that remembering that he is going to be dead soon is the most important instrument he has ever encountered to help me make life's big choices. Because of almost all of these things, all social aspirations, all dignity, all fear of humiliation or defeat, just fall away in the face of death, leaving just what is really necessary.

In order to survive, Jobs had to take on tremendous pressure as the CEO and founder of Apple and create wildly ambitious goods. Jobs relied on the old stoic tradition of considering his death to help bring those fears into context in order to alleviate his fears that these goods and programs would fail. The consequences of errors and mistakes at Apple did not appear as serious or alarming in the light of imminent death. As a result, without being overwhelmed or hampered by fear of disappointment, Jobs was able to concentrate on completing projects.

To brace themselves for defeat, the Stoics used times of harmony and stability.

- **Going Beyond Pleasure**

Stoics advocate voluntary suffering as a greater effort to recognize the positive stuff in one's life. Depriving yourself briefly of things that offer comfort to your life. Without really knowing (e.g., personal car), items that you can quickly become dependent on. Voluntary pain is a simulation of the imminent future, in addition to reminding you of the good stuff in your life, where unexpected events can strip you of the security once considered a norm.

Pleasure comes with a sign of alarm as well. Although happiness is not intrinsically incorrect, the dark side of happiness is often followed by remorse or other kinds of regret. Therefore, if you use cost analysis to treat your impulses for enjoyment, you might understand that forgoing enjoyment creates more pleasure if you weigh in the price of the satisfaction of will-power and guilt.

You are required to put in a lot of time and work to embody Stoicism, which means you will always encounter contradicting influences on the path to

Stoicism; the Stoic ideals you adhere to and your actual actions. Although this is natural, in order to escape frustration, it sits helpful not to confuse Stoic values for your identity. Alternatively, you are advised to establish a stoic spectator.

Your Stoic observer will evaluate and monitor success in your Stoic conduct. The product of Stoic meditation is this inner contact. Stoics examine emotions and previous behavior in order to learn about them, as compared to Buddhist meditation, where you have to let go of your emotions.

Stoic behavior is not intended to be visible. The characteristic of a beginner is to brag about your Stoic principles; true Stoics do not stand out.

One of the most prominent concerns that Stoicism beginners have is, "What luxuries can I avoid?" In fact, they wish to know if, in search of a happier life, stuff like video gaming, gambling, alcohol, and the stuff like this can be avoided. This is a valid issue, but it is the incorrect one, eventually. Stoicism is not about stripping yourself of all you love, contrary to what others may claim. It is not about seeing a mesmerizing sculpture or painting as the colorless mass, or refusing to go out with your friends or eating a delicious meal and tasting nothing.

No, happiness was not seen by the Stoics as anything to be deprived of. If a happy life is the goal, then we need to understand how and when preference, definitely a big element of pleasure, fits into the bigger picture. In accordance with the Stoic conception, the purpose that pleasure plays in life is that it must follow goodness. Without goodness, the pleasures of life are false pits. They are able to make you reliant on their continuous existence and to enslave you.

Life becomes impossible without these joys, leaving you despondent and helpless.

Stoicism is all about providing you with the mental and emotional armor that life inevitably puts you through to protect yourself against the highs and lows. It gives you the assets by which both pleasure and pain can be experienced because if you have not trained yourself to manage them properly, both can lead to ruin. When pleasure is brought into the discussion, in the words of Diogenes Laertius, a well-tamed mind would be able to see pleasure as "indifferent." That is part of the Stoic practitioner's work: to recognize that there is ephemeral enjoyment and pain. What you enjoy can be stripped from you or even used against you.

One thing you do not realize, however, is that Stoic theory has the ability to transform culture and extends way beyond its self-help applications, which only make up just a limited portion of its capacity.

Its simplicity is the essence of Stoicism. It does not make you oblivious to it, despite its demand for indifference towards social status, material goods, and the harsh language of others. Evidently, even the shallowest analysis of the words of Marcus Aurelius is adequate to alter your perceptions, aspirations, and place in the universe. Fear, pain, agony, and misery lose their hold on you, while your ego ceases to be fed by social media exposure and professional accolades. The influence is liberating: as one refuses to dwell on oneself, the energies of the mind are unleashed to follow morality.

For Stoics, life is based on the progression of goodness through goodness alone, embodied as the only true good, righteousness, knowledge, bravery, and self-control. Simply stated, the Stoic pursuits are not prosperity, fitness, prestige, and the possession of material goods. It simply means that everyone may be rich but unhappy. Equally, education, by itself, is not a quality, specifically because deprivation, inevitability, and environmental oppression would be generated by a poor one (where sin is propagated, not necessarily where the standard is dubious). Therefore, the balance of inner isolation and external empathy, and as we note in our open access article, the expression of selfishness by selflessness, is a proper Stoic activity, as Massimo Pigliucci nicely sums up.

Obedience to the Stoic virtues clearly lends itself to a more balanced workplace, school system, and culture in general. The mutual decision to work for self-control, fairness, bravery, and intelligence then feeds off personal change or deterioration. When you imagine a society where the Stoic evils of cowardice, inequality, hypocrisy, and greed rise high and facts are respected less than the presumed importance of the person who utters a hollow counter-argument, this becomes clearer.

We should not believe that it is expected, or appropriate, for a Stoic to treat everyone the same way. In fact, the notion of "circles" of consideration was explored by ancient Stoics like Cicero and Hierocles to express the belief that we instinctively feel a more direct bond with friends and family than we do with others. We must understand, though, that the belief that we both belong to and engage in a cosmopolitan culture of mutual common citizenship is an important characteristic of Stoic philosophy. In particular, Hierocles emphasized the notion that we should put inward circles of consideration to represent the healthier facets of humanity that represent the self and role of self in humanity. This Stoicism, in doing so, provides the basis for a culture that is founded on unity rather than populism.

Stoicism, in this sense, teaches that "obstacle is the path" is not only private it is also a common call to overcome the obstacle together. Now, take a minute to focus on the ability you have to bring change by your investments, including the food in your freezer, the car in your driveway, and the clothing on your back before you find out that social challenges are beyond your grasp. All this stuff means something about you; basically, where you put your dollar or peso is an indication of your beliefs.

You understand that it is your legal duty to challenge the fundamental presumption that it is immediately in your best interest to add (a) and (b) to your possession as you wish to strive towards the Stoic virtue of justice. Whether things (and not virtues) are favored indifferents, at best, (a) and (b), as long as getting them does not become a barrier to your progression towards virtue and (maybe) strengthens your life. At worse, (a) and (b) weaken the road to righteousness when you buy into the systems that produced them by buying them: questionable work conditions in Asian sweatshops and computer factories, the devastation of the South American rainforest, or shady banking transactions in London and New York. That does not infer that the elimination of capitalism is asked for by Stoicism. Indeed, for the Stoics, any dogmatic devotion to capitalism or Marxism, or any unwavering allegiance to the philosophy of the left or right-wing, irrespective of the essence of the views articulated, is unreasonable. This is because there is no political wing of reason or logical thinking, and facts belong to everybody.

- **New Beginnings**

Start living at once, and count each day as a separate life. The Stoics saw possibilities brimming with every day. Know, to fully alter the course of your life requires just a single occurrence, a single conversation.

A bad day does not have to turn into a horrible week. If the fire of anger is not put out, failure to reach a deadline will expand to a rejected business proposal. Where required, the Stoics constructed walls of internal compartmentalization. Small bits in the big picture bind and impact each other. When cancer of rage and negativity is detected, before it grows, it has to be taken out. A blank slate, a fresh day. Before your little failures turn into a big problem, put a halt to the domino effect.

- **Embracing Your Distress**

The Stoics were not unfamiliar with pain like everyone else has walked this planet. It was just as much a part of life in Rome as it is today. The reign of Marcus Aurelius, though the people of Rome loved him, was anything but simple. Civil revolts, wars, pandemics, and financial crises all tested his strength. It would be a preposterous understatement to say that Epictetus suffered early in life: the first three decades were spent in harsh, grinding slavery. He will eternally wear the scars of it.

When their lives took abrupt twists, even the more recent Stoics, including James Stockdale and Viktor Frankl, were both compelled to embody Stoicism. They have suffered much like you are suffering. They battled, just like now you are struggling.

That is because life is not fair. And it is complicated.

But what was unique about the Stoics was that they continued to glow precisely in these tough moments. It was from this hardship that immense importance stemmed from them. James Stockdale spent seven years in a miserable prisoner of war camp. He said that he believed not only that he would get out but also that in the end, he would triumph and turn the experience into my life's defining case, which he would not trade in retrospect.

Crises make us care just about ourselves, how we are hurt, what we are trying to do to survive. But realizing that the whole planet is witnessing the same thing is vital. Marcus gives himself (and us) in Book Six of Meditations in order to keep an important thought in mind. He wrote that frequently meditate on the interconnectedness and reciprocal interdependence of all things in the world. He talks of Sympatheia's Stoic principle, the notion that all things are interwoven together and thus have an affinity with each other. We are meant to support each other and be kind to each other. Sympatheia can supply us with sense when it looks like it is falling apart.

It is unfortunate because, once it is no longer in our hands, so many of us refuse to truly understand the importance of anything. We all take under-appreciate what we have and desperately crave what we do not have. Even Viktor Frankl, who endured horrific massacres in Dachau and Auschwitz for three years, admitted that he, too, took the small stuff for granted. It is the little stuff in difficult times that gives one the sense required to keep working.

We are all guilty of dwelling more on what we need rather than what we do have in times of hardship. Instead of expressing gratitude for the stuff we have not missed yet, we whine. Remember to put your energies into helping people the next time you feel overwhelmed by the state of misery. Do not forget to be happy with what you have. In everything, seek beauty.

- **Strict Honesty**

According to Epicurus, the first step to salvation is an awareness of wrongdoing. There is no urge to be made right for a person who is not conscious that he is doing something wrong. Before you can reform, you have to catch yourself doing it. Show your own remorse, conduct investigations on your own into all the facts against yourself to the best of your abilities. In mitigation, play the first part of the lawyer, then of the judge, and ultimately of the pleader. At times, be rough on yourself.

When you are not sure of why you did not finish your job today and decided to watch Netflix instead, it is hard to change habits.

The urges that prevent us from turning up, participating, committing, and being present are crucial to be aware of. Ask yourself why you feel this way. Get to the bottom of it. Investigate it. Use it as a cue to go ahead anytime you feel resistance. Of course, the trick is teaching yourself to think that way.

It is not a matter of ability or any unconscious reflex. The cultivation of self-awareness of how you think, feel, and respond is a muscle to think through your thoughts. The more you use it, the more it gets better.

These are some of the many stoic practices I will present at your disposal in the next chapters.

Chapter 4 – All the Way to Emotional Resiliency

Stoicism can teach you to get rid of emotional weakness. Remember, your body is an extension of your soul, and Stoicism offers growth of the soul. The theory of Stoic was an invaluable help to the Romans and Greeks, who both lived in a society that was especially brutal in many respects. It is an ancient theory that can be crucial even today, helping you manage the confusion and noise of the world in which we live. Here are some ways Stoicism offers you emotional resilience:

- **Stoic Meditation**

    In the Eastern context, the classic Stoic texts do not usually apply to meditation-that is, as a complete relaxation of one's mind. Classic Stoic meditation is something like a clear-thinking practice.

    Clear thinking suggests that one strives to conceive the situations only as they are in the ups and downs of life. Instead of excessively optimistic rose-colored glasses, or unnecessarily pessimistic dark ones, one sees things as if through transparent eyes.

    Marcus Aurelius writes in his Meditations about being faced by life's clouds or disturbances. They may be big or small. On the road, are there hurdles? Go around them then. Do not ask, 'Why do these things exist?' Although contributing little to one's satisfaction, such investigations or value decisions only disturb the peace of mind.

    Many of the events of existence, of course, are more potentially distressing than hurdles in the road. Aurelius takes a more complicated situation into consideration: you hear that someone is chatting behind your back. It is better to take things at face value from the Stoic viewpoint of Aurelius: sure, everybody is talking about you. But it would not help the peace of mind to speculate further about what precisely the entity is saying, or if this might make them a bad guy, etc.

You should not jump to conclusions like a Stoic or react to anything you hear or see. If you feel that learning more is necessary, you can always ask the individual what they have been talking about you and why. But you might still conclude that it is not worth the hassle and that you would not let your peace of mind shake anyone else's view of you.

Aurelius and other Stoics insisted that it was not the circumstances of life that irritated them. Rather, it is our judgment or assessment of circumstances that worries us, the intricate stories we tell ourselves about encounters. It is not because they pain you, but your own opinion of them, whether you are pained by external things, and it is beyond your power to blot out that opinion now.

In the same way, Epictetus could argue that a human could be in danger and yet happy, sick, and yet happy, dying, and yet happy "by a Stoic mental framing of events.

For the Stoics, the only sanctuary is a well-controlled mind or spirit. Aurelius says in writing about how people often want to get away from it all, to the beach, to the country, to the mountains. You can get away from it whenever you want by going inside. Nowhere you can go to is quieter than your own soul.

Therefore, Stoicism holds that while we cannot always govern events, we can always govern how we think of them. And how we think of them is going to decide whether or not we stay at peace, and therefore happy and prosperous. Cognitive-Behavioral Counseling (CBT) for many years has expected this focus on how we think about situations and how this impacts our feelings and behavior.

In CBT, it is often assumed that how we learn of problems can be regulated and modified. The CBT approach to depression, for instance, holds that negative symptoms (such as intense and enduring sorrow) are at least partially due to the suicidal perception of a maladaptive story we tell ourselves about our lives or situations.

It is often assumed that our feelings about a particular occurrence can be re-shaped or "cognitively restructured," and therefore become less stressed about it. Reflecting on one's death is one Stoic reflection that deserves special notice. This is believed to help us place the ups and downs of life in the right light and to inspire us to make the most use of whatever time we might have.

Let your mortality decide what you do and what you say and think.

In his conversations with the Indian magician Don Juan Matus, Carlos Castaneda wrote a feeling of a memento mori. Don Juan advises Carlos in his Trip to Ixtlan that Death is the only wise counselor we have. This suggests that dreaming about one's eventual demise helps to bring the circumstances about life into perspective and shows what is really important to oneself.

Here are a few meditations that have been put together for you:

1. **A View from Above:** Marcus Aurelius encourages us to do a 'view from above' exercise. This practice allows one to envisage oneself from the third person perspective. In this experience, though keeping ourselves in the center, we zoom

out. We continue to zoom out and ponder the universe's size e.g. your first zoom could involve a view of you from above your house's roof. Increase the magnitude, and you can see your street view, increase the magnitude, and you can see your country's view. Keep going before a glimpse of earth from the stars can be imagined.

Through this view, we will achieve a clearer understanding of the insignificance of our concerns. Whatever problems we might find extremely insignificant relative to the cosmos. When we put things in context, it is much easier to conquer the emotional challenges we face.

2. **Voluntary Discomfort:** Epictetus told us of this exercise. We are going to intentionally put ourselves into stressful conditions in this exercise. In order to prepare ourselves to not cling onto comfort with too great regard, we will do this. Voluntary pain can be carried out in a variety of ways. Some tips are:

   - Exercise in the morning
   - Hot Showers
   - Fasting for one day
   - Walking without a sweater in the winter
   - Slumbering on the floor

Your relationship with ease will change all these things. Life can get much simpler if you resolve the need for warmth. It will be much better to set the targets and adhere to them. This technique is going to harden you up for good.

3. **Negative Visualization:** Despite the term, negative visualization is an activity that, if done regularly, will improve the default level of satisfaction. The practice

consists of you thinking what it would be like if you lost certain things in your life. Any of the things during the workout that you might think are:

- How it feels to lose your social standing.
- How not to have a roof over your head would feel.
- How it would be to live in a country in the third world.
- How it would feel for a loved one to suffer.
- How it would be to have a physical handicap.

The aim of this exercise is not to be gloomy or morbid; it is to put things in perspective. Allowing you to see how genuinely lucky you are. It also trains you for situations in the worst condition in which one of these things occurs. You are not supposed to dwell on these ideas, but from time to time, remember them.

Naturally, as you accept items being withdrawn from your life, you tend to develop a sense of appreciation. This is a very realistic way for you to exercise appreciation. Gratitude is necessary now because of a thing called 'hedonic adaptation'; literally, it is a concept that describes the propensity for people to often return to their default happiness level.

Your base level of satisfaction will grow for a while if you win the lotto and become a millionaire. However, you can revert to your base stage as you get used to the lifestyle, amid all the expensive gadgets. Gratitude breaks this cycle, causing each step up the ladder to be celebrated. When you own a box, you can be grateful, and when you own a Lamborghini, you can be grateful.

- **Avoid Impossible Hope**

    The Stoics would not advise you to cheer up or be cheerful if you are down because life gets tough. You have never been told to be more optimistic.

    They were simply propagating the reverse.

    They believed that you were not supposed to have hope for the future, but rather eliminate hope. To the stoics, the heroin of feelings was hope-the higher you are raised, the lower you fell.

    Stoics also warn you that horrible stuff is going to happen. Your vehicle might get stolen, you might go to prison, but it is going to be all right. They are trying to tell you your life is full of misfortune and that you are going to get through everything. They claimed that the result of incorrect decisions is negative emotions. That our expectations of life are false and that we needed to behave in compliance with life.

    A healthy mental state, for the stoics, is determined by its potential for reason and goodness. A unanimous conviction in the stoic culture is that emotion should not motivate us only logic and reason. This does not mean absolutely stamping out the feelings.

    It means getting the thoughts out of the driver's seat and putting them in the passenger seat. The belief in living in harmony with nature is perhaps problematic in our hedonistic modernity. This suggests that food is solely for life, and wellbeing and sex is just for reproduction.

They thought you might end up being possessed by the ownership of material goods. Buying more things can only add to the fear that these things will be preserved.

Their conviction in suicide is perhaps more divisive. They thought a man should be able to take his own life. In fact, when his student, and now Emperor Nero, asked Seneca to commit suicide, he did not bat an eye. As his wife and children hold onto him weeping, he declared confidently, why is the need to cry over parts of life? All of life calls for tears.

- **Accepting Fate**

Friedrich Nietzsche popularized the idea of embracing one's destiny around 1882 when he invented the Latin word, Amor fati. The theory, however, goes back farther, and the Stoics, thoroughly realizing what was and was not within their influence, made embracing one's destiny or Amor fati, a cornerstone of their philosophy.

Epictetus uses the example of a bath to explain embracing one's destiny in the Enchiridion, curated by his pupil Arrian:

When you take some initiative, remind yourself of the purpose of the initiative. If you are trying to bathe, imagine the things that normally happen in the bathroom: some people spill water, some kick, and some use abusive words. Thus, if you say to yourself, "I will now go bathe and keep my own consciousness in a state consistent with nature," and in the same way with respect to any other action, you will go through this action more comfortably. For, therefore, if some difficulty emerges in bathing, you would have it ready to say, it was not only to bathe that you needed but to keep your mind in a nature-conforming state; and if you are troubled with things that happen, you will not keep it.

The Dichotomy of Power, which is the Stoic tenet of knowing what is and is not under one's power, is part of this notion of embracing one's destiny. The objects beyond our influence, Epictetus thought, are:

- Pursuit
- Opinions
- Aversion
- Desire
- Our own acts

Things claimed by Epictetus were not under our influence are:

- Property
- Body
- Command
- Reputation
- Whatever our own acts are not

Therefore, fate is not something in our hands, and it contains components of existence that we have only "partial" hands over; that is what the Stoics categorized as "not being in our control."

Among the other Stoics, Marcus realized that he was in control of himself, of his actions, and of his effect on the world. But other than that, the universe itself and the actions of others have no influence over him. Therefore, while writing in book two of Meditations, he places himself to take advantage of his situation.

It is now time to understand the essence of the world of which you belong, and to the governing force to which you are the offspring; and to understand that your time does have a limit to it. Then use it to progress your enlightenment; else, it will vanish and never again be in your power.

Marcus reminds himself of the influence he has inside himself, that his time on earth is restricted, but that he is a part of a much greater image regardless of what he does and pursues, over which he actually does not have complete control.

During the times of the Stoics, embracing one's destiny was important, as many of the Stoics whose works endure today, such as Epictetus, Seneca, and Musonius Rufus, preached philosophy under emperors who were decisive in their assessments and made cut-second decisions that caused the intellectual community to reverberate. At some point in their hard life, each of the above-named intellectuals finds himself exiled.

Emperor Claudius banished Seneca from Rome in 41 AD.

Epictetus, banished by Emperor Domitian from Rome.

Musonius Rufus, like all intellectuals of the time, was banished from Rome in 71 AD by Emperor Vespasian.

All three had to let go of their lives and travel, giving up everything that they had, including their right to live the life that they wanted to live.

They reminded themselves to be present at the moment and to embrace the life-given events.

- **Momento Mori**

As this phenomenon is briefly described above, just think of yourself as dead. Your life has been lived by you. Take what is left now to live it properly. The legend goes that a star-struck crowd will be cheered on after a famous battle general walking triumphantly through ancient Rome. With the general saying the words 'Memento mori'-which translates as remember thou art mortal -a slave will walk side by side.

For a second, think about it. How different everything would be if someone else muttered 'you're going to die' every time we were told how wonderful we would be in a sales pitch? Or while we count the likes of our selfies? Or when a long-overdue promotion is awarded? When we are continually reminded of our mortality, how much more modest and graceful we can walk through life.

The thought that we could die too is pretty depressing for all of us. It makes us mad about our humanity. But instead of saying that life is too short, listen to one of the fathers of Stoicism, Seneca, who said:

"Life, if you know how to use it, is long."

The Stoics knew that it was an essential road to happiness to come to terms with death, rather than being defined by it. We should then use our impending mortality as the driving philosophy, giving it a sense of intent and priority, to live a more fulfilling and fruitful existence.

And if you ever think about death, note that a long time before you were born, you were dead. Back then, it was not all that bad, was it?

- **Premeditatio malorum**

As this phenomenon is briefly described above, Premeditatio malorum advises you to constantly watch out for what could go wrong, roughly translated as prepare for all evils. It is a pessimistic lesson in imagination that forces you to imagine everything that could go south. It is outstanding as a mental tool, and it trains you for the many challenges of life.

But you do not have to shut yourself off from what could be considered as negative consequences in order to actually live a healthy life and become happy, whatever the concept of success is.

And while planning for the worse cannot do anything to modify the worse, your endurance is educated. You will be much more able to cope with them as difficult situations arise. Premeditatio malorum helps you to keep your nerve instead of being blown off track by circumstances when you have already agreed on the path ahead beforehand.

With those who know about Cognitive Behavioral Therapy (CBT), this notion about planning for the worse will ring a bell. Indeed, CBT therapists frequently encourage their clients to constantly imagine fearful occurrences as if they had already occurred as part of a strategy called mental habituation. Clients become more successful in controlling their fear and think less about the future by teaching them to confront certain events in a controlled way.

It is an alarming sign. It may be delusional to only wish for the future, but it is also catastrophic and too much pessimistic thought. A stoical approach to loving your destiny allows you to look at all angles at events and performance, both positive and negative. Then, the general position becomes that of neutrality.

Ryan Holiday neatly puts it as expecting a fun filled and fruitful day. Be ready just in case it is not.

- **The Obstacle is the Way**

Stoicism encourages one to accept and respond to hardship with a feeling of lightness and even cheerfulness.

In reality, in spite of the morbid touch, the Stoics are quite a positive group. They assume that any negative has an equivalent and the opposite, flipping the concept of premeditatio malorum on its head. Any negative is, therefore, a positive.

We should accept challenges according to Stoic teachings and see them as chances to exercise some of the Stoic virtues of justice, charity, religion, hope, courage, temperance, and prudence.

They inspire us, not in spite of what's before us, but because of it, to treat any drama as an opportunity to succeed. By wanting less, by letting go of all the foolish assumptions you have accumulated in your self-absorbed existence, by forgetting about happiness and realizing that anything important in this universe needs hardship and compromise, you will live a more rewarding and meaningful life.

Of course, we are humans. So, even as we want to turn up as our best selves in our decision-making, some unreasonable impulses will probably play havoc.

By holding our thoughts in balance and being steady, the best way to fight is this point of view.

That does not mean throwing aside negative thoughts and emotions or dismissing them. Our thoughts, on the contrary, are an important part of who we are, and we do not wish to be apathetic or neglect our capacity to feel anything.

Instead, Stoics advocate equanimity-calmness and patience that helps you to balance yourself and not panic. It is a sense of poise that keeps you from being blinded by passion. You lose the anchor and become anchored instead of being swept up by the wind. You then ask yourself: Does panicking bring something positive to this situation at this moment?

Historian

Ada Palmer speaks about the development of an inner fortress as if she sees her concentrating on something that upsets me, and she has a kind of triage of reactions. She asks herself (A) Is it possible to find an actionable answer to the issue? If not (B), will she get me to stop worrying and let go of the issue? Is it possible for her to ask herself if this would matter in a year or five years?

Challenges are nothing more than an ability to exercise some virtue like persistence, modesty, bravery, resourcefulness, fairness, reason, and imagination. The three disciplines are dependent on each other.

1. **Persistence:** It is how we see and realize what is going on around us, and what those events would mean is what we decide—a root of power or of great weakness, maybe our expectations. We only add to our problems if we are subjective, emotional, and short-sighted. We must, as the ancient people

practiced, learn how to limit our impulses and their influence over our lives in order to avoid being consumed by the world around us. To swat away the parasites of bad expectations, to distinguish accurate messages from false ones, to root out bias, anticipation, and anxiety requires discipline talent. But it is worth it because the reality is what is left. While others are scared or excited, we will keep calm and undisturbed. Straightforwardly and simply, we will see things as they actually are, neither good nor evil. In the fight against challenges, this would be an enormous advantage for us.

2. **Action:** Action is commonplace; appropriate action is not. It is not any kind of conduct, as a discipline, that can do, but guided conduct. In the service of the whole, everything must be completed. We will dismantle the barriers in front of our step by step, action by action. We will behave in the best interest of our priorities with persistence and versatility. Action requires bravery, imaginative application, not brashness, and not brute strength. Our movements and choices characterize us: with boldness, deliberation, and determination, we must be sure to act. Such are the virtues of correct and good conduct: nothing more, no feeling, avoidance, or assistance from others. Action is the solution to our predicaments and the cure.

3. **Will:** Will is our inner force, which the outer world can never influence. It is our last card for a trump. If action is what we rely on when we still have some agency in our situation, when the agency has all but gone, the will is what we rely on. Placed in a situation that appears and undeniably and unchangeable destructive, we should turn it into an experience of growth, a humbling experience, and an ability to provide others with warmth. That is the strength of will. Yet it must be cultivated. Even in dark days, we must brace for hardship and chaos, master the art of acquiescence, and cultivate cheerfulness. People too much believe that, that is how awful we want anything to be. In fact, with defeat, the will has much more

to do than with power. True will is quiet strength, modesty, and flexibility. Weakness masked by ambition and bluster is the other type of will.

- **Eradicate Ego**

    Modesty is the secret to achievement, but to know that some deity-awful people are doing well in life, you do not have to go too hard.

    The ego can be a strong but unreliable driver of success. It will caress you on a good day, whispering that you are invincible and better than anyone else. It would bury you with pain on a bad day.

    Stoicism acknowledges that when it comes to being popular, having a big ego will also be useful. But it also admits that by sacrificing your character and your spirit, you pay the price.

    Stoics claim, close to Buddhists, the ego reveals itself as an exaggerated sense of self-importance. It keeps us from possessing the modesty to realize that we know only a limited proportion of what we need to know. This keeps us from learning.

    It is what the popular rich ones know most deep down but find it hard to accept that we are not as incredible as we think we are. We applaud ourselves for becoming the room's smartest individual. Alternatively, we should be wondering why we were too frightened to associate ourselves in the first place with more knowledgeable individuals.

    Ryan Holiday puts it as the ego is the enemy of what you desire and have: the supremacy of art of working for others well, of true imaginative insight, of building loyalty and assistance, of lifespan, of repeating your performance and sustaining it. This discourages incentives and prospects. This is a magnet for rivals and failures.

As author James Clear said that the surest way to keep yourself from knowing a subject is to assume that you know it already.

These stoic practices will help you become mentally strong by keeping your emotions under control and have a logical approach towards everyday problem-solving.

Chapter 5 – Get Rid of Stress, Trauma, Fear & Anger

When I said Stoicism is a way of life, I meant it. It is not something philosophical you will read in this book and forget in a week as you find no relevance of it in your life. It is the cure to the obstacles that impede you in living a healthy and happy life. Stoicism holds the key to solving real-life problems like stress, trauma, fear, anger, and greed. These issues of the mind will not let you have a peaceful life to fulfill your purpose of birth. I have put together the ways to deal with all of these problems and even disabilities. You will know, the body is an extension of your soul. You need to purify your soul to have a purified bodily experience. Let's get started:

5.1 Stoic Ways of Getting Out of Stress

In our lives, we all have stressors. They are so many or so strong at times that they can seem daunting. So, if you would like your life to be better, that is fully understandable. But the wish is vain at the same time. What life throws at you, you cannot control. You will not avoid stressors from invading your life, no matter what you do.

However, all you should do is determine how you want to view them. Wisely and rationally, you can opt to respond to the stressors. And you can learn in the end how to survive even in the face of uncertainty.

When we look at what constitutes "stress," we discover that it is an undue, exaggerated, or inappropriate response to a situation. Not only can stress have detrimental consequences on the psyche, but it also affects our physical wellbeing and may contribute to decreased effectiveness, disability, and occasionally death.

It is extremely crucial that we continue to assess our lives to see where we are, with the understanding that possible health conditions exist and can be triggered by stress. Are we late with regarding certain payments? Are our present relationships impacting our mental clarity? Are our unnecessary obligations wearing us down?

Here are a few ways to get rid of stress:

1. **Creating a Gratitude List:** Gratitude is believed to raise our "feel-good" hormones in the body. Not only does our whole day shift as we write what we are thankful for, but by seeing the benefits of our lives, we are able to truly understand the people and things around us. This trains the mind to actively seek what is beneficial, thus reducing the level of stress.

2. **Keeping Anxiety Down:** You may be worried about what you have done, what you have not done, or what you ought to do. It could be a previous 'failure,' a poor interview, relationship, public humiliation, or worse yet some sort of physical or emotional violence. While always letting it hurt you, you might be 'running away' from the past. Yet the distinction of those that are under our power and other those that are not under our power is one of the core concepts of Stoicism. Nothing from the past you can change. Will you have power over stuff that has happened already? Of course, the answer is no.

We then have to embrace the experience happily and refuse to let it have any effect on us now. What is done is in the past. We only have so many resources and effort to draw in a day, so why waste it on the uncontrollable events? These ideas of the past are also just impressions; these impressions are not facts; they need not to be viewed as such.

What Seneca was talking about is the extraordinary opportunity we have to decouple our cognition as human beings. Decoupled Cognition is our capacity to reflect on something that has occurred or will occur while also remaining mindful of our surroundings. It also covers our desire, within our own minds, to have a dynamic relationship with another human (even an abstract one) at another time and location. We may also place ourselves "inside others," wondering what they think and how they will react to us. We can see how valuable this talent is for social engagement and planning, but it is also the root of all our woes.

We have come to be in a constant state of decoupled cognition-in the current moment, never ever being. How much do we really immerse ourselves either in the past or the future in activities at hand without 'one eye'? How much do we have discussions with people while not even listening or moving the car, and don't even remember the journey until we get to our destination? Typically, this loss of understanding is because we are so busy being worried about the past/future or upset or hankering that we do not really realize what it truly is like to be present, just-be.

No man limits his sadness to the present. If we are continuously trying to get the attention to the present moment, our mindfulness will increase; unhappiness and fear will be difficult to take control over us.

The future lies within the domain of things we cannot control, as, in the past, things are not under our' power.' It makes us understand how pointless it is to spend some time thinking or dreaming about it, clearly making us realize that the future is indeed uncertain. Hope and fear are the same. Both of them are the 'enemy of the present moment,' and we should always understand that any enemy of the present moment is our enemy.

It is clear how it can make one nervous about dreading the future at the moment, but optimism is even more complex, more cunning in the way it can create uncertainty and trigger unhappiness. Hoping for the future leads one to wish things to unfold in a certain manner and, therefore, to live a life in contrast to amor fati. It is also this wish and optimism that truly leads us to fear over those effects, triggering our anxiety. Remember, Amor fati and consider doing what you can for what you have right now and survive at the moment.

3. **Distinguishing Pain and Suffering:** Pain is a part of life that is inevitable. Suffering is voluntary, though. The initial reaction that you have to a hurtful incident is pain. Suffering is what happens when you contribute to the suffering in your imagination.

For example, assume that you have broken your leg. Your discomfort stems from tissue that is hurt. Your suffering is the result of your thoughts about pain. "This agony is bad. What if it does not ever go away? Perhaps I will never ever be able to walk properly? Anxious thoughts like these can add your pain to a tremendous amount of suffering.

So, pay heed to the mind's plot. Do not forget that thoughts are not facts. And it is within the power to choose whether or not to trust them. And it is within the power to choose whether or not to trust them. Yes, you are in agony, but all that you really know is that only needless misery will be added to build stories of what the agony could cause.

I hope these three methods help you overcome stress. Trauma will be the subject of the next section.

5.2 Stoic Ways of Getting Out of Trauma

Stoicism notes that, in order to thrive, we need only to restore our character to nature again, rather than to stay prisoner to the distortions absorbed from stressful events, as well as by society and culture. Our approach to trauma distorts our identity, such that it is no longer in accordance with nature. This suggests that we are not able to be normal or function normally.

Stoicism claims that by keeping our character according to nature, we thrive. The character may discern good from bad and behave accordingly. Nature would teach us if we would just look, how to discern, and behave. Note how distinct this teaching is from that of the popular culture of all ages, which claims that outward objects can make us prosper, such as possessions and humans. Stoicism maintains that external objects, unless we use them to create a character, do not help us thrive.

The fact that external things will help us prosper is one of the major fallacies of our civilization. Remember all the ads that every day bombard us. But, above all, trauma survivors know that money or land does not make us happy. It is better to have them, but they do not make us happy because we are still within our broken self at the end of the day, and we live with our constraints.

We need to restore our character in harmony with nature in order to prosper. If we use them to restore our character, external things may be beneficial. An important contributing factor to our struggle to succeed is that we have trouble differentiating between good and bad. Our responses to stressful experiences distort our processes of reasoning so that we contend with what is positive and what is evil. This happens on top of the regular distortions that society and culture present to us.

Stoicism claims that only goodness, virtuous acts, and moral excellence are "good." Vice versa (immorality) and acts driven by vice are the only "bad." "Neither good nor bad, something external" is "indifferent." It hinges on our actions.

Note the contrast between the Stoic and other societies' thoughts. The moral world is categorized by most societies into two categories: good and bad. It is divided into good and poor plus "indifferent" by Stoicism. I have described this before. Now let's discuss it in accordance with trauma.

Even before we came across trauma, our dualistic culture showed us an unconstructive way of thinking about good and bad. Society says that some external factors are good, such as income or families, and those other external things, such as poverty or low social status, are poor.

Stoicism, however, asserts that moral excellence is the only good thing and immorality is the only bad thing. And the rest is neutral. Chocolate fudge sundaes, while they are not calorically neutral, are socially neutral! Those thoughts and acts turn evil, not the chocolate or the fudge, or the ice cream shop if you cannot stop dreaming about them and buy one every day after work.

Note carefully that Stoicism means that we are inner of good and bad: it falls into our character; external objects are neutral, implying that they are not good or evil, but simply indifferent.

This tiny difference has enormous repercussions. Let's just discuss it.

We are conditioned by culture to separate external things into positive or evil (in total contrast to the state of nature). Stoicism, though, notes that they are neutral. Both external objects are oblivious to you, neither good nor evil. Wealth is not good or evil, either. Poverty is neither evil nor good. Neither good nor evil is family. Death is neither evil nor good. It is a normal phase.

Stoicism suggests that only "preferred" or "dispreferred" are certain external, indifferent items. They are "preferred indifferent," health, money, friends, families, etc. These are not "good;" they are the items to which our virtuous acts (or vice) are directed. "Dispreferred indifferent" are the things such as disease, hunger, death, alienation from society, etc. Sickness is not bad: it is an occurrence of good or sin to which we direct.

For trauma patients, this sort of thought has consequences.

Is it bad / evil, then, that you have PTSD (Post Traumatic Stress Disorder)? Stoicism says no; this is a morally neutral, despised experience, to which either goodness (good thoughts and actions) or sin (bad thoughts and actions) may be guided. As a human phenomenon, PTSD is an external, neutral thing: if you do not allow it, it will not affect your character.

I hope you understand now that you have to conquer the guilt to be able to see PTSD and the incidents that led to it as neutral things that are simply disliked. The next section will be about living a peaceful life without fear.

5.3 Stoic Ways of Getting out of Fear

It is a timeless fact that a lot of the things we are concerned about never happen. Yet our imagined fears may have actual repercussions. Fear will distort your reality and will distort your perception and confuse what is actually going on, like other intense emotions such as rage. Fear's grasp can be paralyzing.

Think Like a Stoic

How can you get the control back? How do you get back to your successful self-ready to face the obstacle that comes next?

First of all, one of the most important rituals of the Stoic tradition must begin: the pre-meditation. What is the worst thing that could go wrong? Study it. Feel it in the skin and bones. Understand what it is going to sound like and taste. When you are done, you will have lost the suspense and some of the fear. You have gotten yourself comfortable for the worst. The man who has expected the coming of trouble, as Seneca put it best, takes away their strength as they arrive.

Now prepare yourself. What will you do to brace yourself? When the worst-case emerges, what choices do you have? How do you prevent the existence of it? To reduce the likelihood of the worse happening, what will you do today? How would you bounce back if it happens? On paper, write it all down and work about it. These moves are the main instruments in the "fear environment" exercise of bestselling author and entrepreneur Tim Ferriss, inspired by Stoicism, clarified your worries, imagining the worst-case scenario, coming up with ideas, and strategizing to avoid anything that might come.

Think of Cato, one of the worlds' most leading stoics, wandering about barefoot and in scant clothes in hot and cold. About why? For a life in which he would have to endure hardship, he was educating himself. He was a Roman aristocrat, of course; he would certainly never have been penniless. But he did not want to dread it at all, so he led a penniless life, in brief intervals. And that basic exercise gave him an unusual strength, the opportunity to experience and plan for and learn about a dilemma that stripped him of all his strength.

Military men know how to shoot to kill, but why are they preparing to be on the gunfire's receiving end? The same explanation that a corporation is doing "war gaming" against its rivals. Football players perform fumble recovery for the same purpose of giving reps to their replacement quarterback. You will reduce your fear when you can research and learn about what has failed in the past or brace for what may fail in the future.

Night and day, firefighters prepare to get into burning houses. Police officers fire hundreds of bullets at firing ranges to ensure that when a situation occurs, they are ready. Special operators around the world prepare for hostage rescue scenarios, carrying out the distant likelihood of an enemy catching one of our own over and over again.

Preparing for what may come is how you realize that you are able to enter a situation filled with confusion and turmoil. You have done your best to train. You take care of the fear in this way.

Think of practice as immunity to weakness; immunity to fear; immunity to your own, and hesitation and doubt. Practice what you do not think you can do, and you can discover you have more potential than you thought possible.

In brief, this is the blueprint that you require to take power over fear: In brief, this is the blueprint that you require to take power over fear:

1. Write down that. Just sense it.
2. Inquire if you can stop it.
3. Practice eliminates fear: do whatever is required to realize that for all your effort, you have steadied yourself and prepared.

Let me assert this strong conviction that fear itself is the only thing we have to fear. It is an irrational, nameless, unjustified dread that paralyzes required attempts to transform withdrawal into advance. The Stoics knew that, regardless of the suffering it caused, terror was to be hated. In contrast to the harm we do to ourselves and others as we unthinkingly scramble to stop them, the things we fear pale. An economic downturn is bad; turmoil is worse. Terror does not help a difficult situation; it just makes things worse.

The next section will be about controlling the biggest devil of all evil; anger.

5.4 Stoic Ways of Getting Out of Anger

If you learn how to let go of the rage, you will have conquered the wildest of feelings and will find it far easier to handle other states of mind. But even though you do not think you have a big rage problem, read on as you are going to discover more useful emotional intelligence insights. Marcus Aurelius tried notoriously to control his own temper. In his novel, he returns to this topic time and time again as he tells himself of different ideas that he has found useful in handling frustration. He also mentions stoic anger control tactics at one point. He explained them as "gifts from Apollo," meaning the healing deity. Five of them are here:

1. It is not the behavior that irritates you; it is your thoughts on it.

    This is one of Stoicism's most basic precepts and coping techniques. When it occurs in different situations or is handled by different persons, are you still similarly offended by the same behavior? Are other people similarly mad as they witness the kind of stuff that gets you upset? It is arguable because they have varying views and perceptions about the situation if there is any difference in the way people react. Ultimately, it is our moral assessments that decide how mad we are over something that reaches us in life. So, according to the Stoics, it is worth having that in mind and then asking whether we place too much emphasis on items within our direct control.

2. Mind that you are also not perfect.

The Stoics felt that acknowledging our own shortcomings was crucial for us. Stop and ask yourself if anyone offends you, if you may do certain things yourself, or at least have the ability to do things that others might find objectionable. As therapists tend to say, when you point a finger to accuse another person, you should remember the three fingers on the very same hand pointed in your own direction. Confessing that we are guilty of committing equivalent crimes to someone we are angry with will also alleviate our indignation, allowing us to think more rationally at the situation.

3. Your rage does more damage to you than what you are upset at.

This is a very common Stoic doctrine, too. Our traits are blurred by rage, which the Stoics claim appears grotesque and unnatural. However, it also distorts our brains by clouding our capacity to think. Anger is all transient insanity, they claim. The acts of other people only affect outward objects, our prestige, our possessions, or even our physical bodies, but our own wrath, according to the Stoics, ultimately hits deeper by harming our moral character. By stressing about what it costs us, we will also lose the grip rage on our minds: the detrimental effects of indulging in it.

4. Do not stoop to the level of them. React with compassion to rage.

The Stoics have sought to promote a better alternative way of looking at stuff, in addition to questioning their own feelings of frustration. Stoicism is simply an ideology that is really humane. Rage, according to them, is usually based on the conviction that something wrong has been done by others, and they deserve to be punished. The contrary will be the conviction that they need to be supported or may be informed. Marcus said that when he was upset by the aggressive actions of another human, after discussing his own feelings of rage, he would kindly take them aside and explain to them, without condescension, why they were only hurting themselves rather than him.

5. Accept the probability that they just do not understand why something is wrong.

The striking but divisive doctrine that no man intentionally does evil was taught by Socrates. Marcus states that when questioned, everyone excuses their actions; we all get upset if we are told that we are doing something morally wrong. Even Stalin and Hitler's monsters thought what they were doing was justified. In their own heads, criminals who know that what they are doing is wrong, always find reasons to justify that. Ancient thinkers rigorously discussed ethics with everyday people because they became very familiar with the ways in which we confused ourselves on what was right and wrong. Relatively uncertain about life, we are both. In a way to temper his frustration with people, Marcus tells himself of this.

The treasure of knowledge gifted to us by Marcus surely has the power to scare the evil of anger away. Next, we will talk about greed.

5.5 Stoic Ways of Getting Out of Greed

One of the darker elements in Roman history is the brutality of the mob. There was an angry crowd which, during the time of Marius, tore Saturninus to bits. The grieving, angry citizens, were there who, riled up by the funeral prayer of Mark

Antony after Caesar's death, assassinated the poet Cinna just because he had the same name as one of the accomplices.

It is frightening what a group of people can do when civil society's unwritten rules break down. Perhaps there is no better day than Black Friday in America to think about this. Fresh off the gratefulness of Thanksgiving, by greedily gorging on stuff, we decide to reward ourselves.

A day whose entire purpose is in larger conflict with the Stoic concept of sympathy is difficult to think of. The same individuals who previously sat in a peaceful manner with their family are now ready to engage in hand-to-hand fighting over a flat-screen television deal. Instead of enjoying the time off, at lower and lower prices, individuals were lined up for hours in the cold season to buy more and more nonsense they did not actually need. Not to replace the nonsense they purchased last Black Friday, but to add to the stack. The only expense that Black Friday shoppers do not mind paying for those savings? Countless traffic accidents, yelling matches, and retail employees' collateral damage are trampled to death.

"What's bad for the hive is bad for the bee," as Marcus wrote in Meditations. It's difficult to argue that Black Friday is good for anything or anyone but the big business bottom line. So, it would be great if you spent this morning thinking about the larger picture, the biggest picture, instead of following the general public on a shopping spree and possibly a killing spree.

Since we are all human, all are part of the same greater body, and we should be humane to each other. We come from the same soil, and one day we will each return to it the same way. Not only does it affect other people because we forget this, it mourns many millions, but it still hurts us.

Marcus Aurelius teaches us to revere the gods and take care of one another. That is what sympathy is about. Oikeiôsis, love with your fellow human beings, is about that. We ought to live it every day, honestly, but today we ought to be particularly conscious of it.

As the exact opposite of the Black Friday sale, at Daily Stoic, we sell our Sympatheia coins at the full retail price before 6 a.m. on Monday, 2 December. But, if you purchase one, we are going to give you another one free of charge to give to a family member, friend, or colleague who might benefit from it.

As we launch the holiday season, as you struggle with demanding in-laws, travel delays, or queues, and long lines, we hope you have this idea in mind. Don't let you get infected with the new spirit of selfishness and materialism. Alternatively, we must all rely on assurances that we are not alone, that we are part of something greater than ourselves, that we all owe a responsibility to a greater good, over and above our own selfish needs and wishes.

All of us are interconnected and united and made for each other. The Stoics understood it. The Buddhists understood it, and so do we. Never can this reality be far from our heads.

5.6 Stoic Ways of Getting Out of Disabilities

The ancient philosophy of Stoicism is still massively crucial today, many western philosophers and health practitioners' claim.

The key to a calm mind lies in being honest about what we can and cannot control in our lives, according to the Stoics. Some aspects are actually out of our grasp, and when attempting to alter them, we cannot waste resources. We should plan to come into hard times and welcome them.

According to Stoicism, tragedy is all part of existence and is simply acknowledged instead of going on. That is really well, you would say, but what about those people out there who are still struggling, day after day? Those with debilitating illnesses, fear, injuries, sadness, and sorrow?

And when our children are the ones who suffer, it is much harder to make sense of it. As parents, protecting our children is our responsibility, and it is so challenging to see them face the daily struggles that their disabilities offer. The sadness we feel for them is very genuine, as is the remorse for the life they are supposed to have had. Is it not human and completely reasonable to grieve and to experience sorrow and sadness when our loved ones have experienced something very bad?

Yes, absolutely, in my experience. And getting stuck in this mentality is also very easy. 'It's not right; he did not deserve this. It should never have happened.' And to feel anger towards the racism and lack of acceptance that people display so much in the rest of the country. It is not shocking that parents feel so disconnected from certain special needs and that they and their children are 'hard-to-do' to meet all these difficulties.

It is enough to make one bitter for a lifetime, to remain in a constant state of bitterness and remorse, and to reflect endlessly on the injustice served by creation.

Can a stoic attitude be beneficial for parents of autistic children? Some of us are simply too drained to find solutions, strategies for coping; we simply work. It can feel like a miracle to only get through another day. We cannot help but think, 'what choice do we have when we are lauded for our strength and endurance, or even for how stoic we are? The Stoics taught, without bias or expectation, that we should see things as they are.

The Stoics taught, without bias or expectation, that we should see things as they are. This technique allows us to recognize what cannot be improved, to take steps when we can, and to press on to conquer our challenges with bravery and determination. When we are not overwhelmed by negative thoughts and judgments on how it should be, this is much better.

When applying to raise a child with disabilities is clearly not an easy philosophy. The truth remains that multiple challenges need to be addressed. It feels like an uphill fight and a relentless war all too much. It is really hard not to draw assumptions as to how things should have been.

Yet we do need a language to live by, instruments to help us make sense of it all and to help us manage the minefield while attempting to ensure that our own needs and our children's needs are fulfilled.

Stoicism does not mean that we should shake off our problems, and it does not mean that we should not experience our discomfort. More than that, we learn to let go of the bad aspects we cling to, tensions and resentment. To keep our thoughts organized and regulated so that with resilience and inner-stability, we can face those challenges. This is definitely something worth reaching for.

There appears to be a widespread myth that the grim and unemotional Stoics is. Sensing and overcoming thoughts is not the same as not experiencing them. So, for those out there who are facing a less common life, indeed, it is real that we have the work of a lifetime ahead of us. Perhaps we can begin to find more inner peace if we can continue to face the day-to-day struggles using the cardinal virtues alluded to by the Stoics (bravery, wisdom, and self-discipline, and morality.)

The practice of Stoicism may be particularly useful to those suffering from lifelong physical disabilities. The sense of a loss of physical agency may cause individuals to feel that they have lost all control over their lives. Stoicism may teach impaired people to accept their situation and recalibrate their life goals. Stoicism encourages one to think about what we can do instead of dwelling on what we do not do.

This was the stoic approach to stress, anger, greed, fear, trauma, and disabilities.

Chapter 6: Stoicism & Mindfulness

Life can be overbearing. Our heads are overflowed with chatter, our worldview is corrupted and skewed, and our capacity to be present is lost.

Sometimes, life is frantic and exhausting. And our happiness, health, schooling, jobs, and even the economy are influenced by it.

It is a world that is noisy. While keeping one eye on the children and another on the screen, you fold the laundry. When listening to the radio and driving to work, you prepare your day and then arrange your weekend. But you may find yourself losing your link to the present moment in a rush to complete necessary things, missing out on what you are doing and how you feel. Have you found whether this morning you feel well-rested or the forsythia is in bloom along your way to work?

There is increasing awareness that treatments focused on mindfulness provide treatment for our mental health. A somewhat less well-known fact is that our physical well-being is also greatly enhanced by these methods.

Mindfulness takes us beyond surviving and making do. The strategies allow one to see the world differently; to evolve, thrive, and live a more caring and fulfilling life.

Mindfulness is the process of keeping the attention on the current moment consciously and embracing it without judgment. Mindfulness is now being clinically studied and has been discovered to be a crucial factor in minimizing depression and enhancing general satisfaction.

To further emphasize the importance of mindfulness, here are a few benefits it carries:

- Growing your mindfulness potential encourages multiple attitudes that lead to a satisfying life. Being aware makes it possible to savor life's rewards as they unfold, lets you become actively involved in tasks and provides a better opportunity to cope with adverse events. Many people who practice mindfulness find that they are less likely to get wrapped up with worries about the future or remorse about the past by reflecting on the here and now, are less obsessed with worries about progress and self-esteem, and are more able to establish deep ties with others.

- Psychotherapists have turned to mindfulness therapy in recent years as a significant part of the treatment of a variety of topics, including drug abuse, depression, eating disorders, anxiety disorders, disputes between partners, and obsessive-compulsive behavior.

- If overall well-being is not enough of a motivation, scientists have shown that in a variety of ways, mindfulness strategies tend to enhance physical health. Mindfulness can help manage heart disease, alleviate stress, decrease blood pressure, improve sleep, decrease chronic pain, and alleviate stomach issues.

Now let's discuss where mindfulness comes into play in Stoicism.

Stoic Mindfulness

Buddhism and Stoicism have a lot in common while still possessing ample distinctions to give the practitioner, who is versed in one practice, pause for thought when meeting the other. Both Stoicism and Buddhism are strongly realistic philosophies with an emphasis on the here and now, especially in their more modern 'engaged' and non-renunciant types. Marcus Aurelius, the Roman Empire's emperor, whose private metaphysical diary the Meditations was saved, writes that only in this present moment does each man exist. Anything that has since been encountered or lies in confusion. One needs to be mindful that we are here right now that the present moment is the only moment to be alive. The advice given by Marcus Aurelius resonates with the Buddhist practitioner that your mind carefully focuses every hour on the success of the mission on hand, with human compassion, dignity, and liberty and benevolence, and puts all other thoughts aside. If you conduct each operation as if it were the last one, you will accomplish this.

It is not surprising, in this sense, that anything closely analogous to 'mindfulness' occupies a central position within Stoicism. It is called prosoche, which can be interpreted as 'attention' by Epictetus, the ex-slave whose lessons survive in a concise handbook Encheiridion and volumes of the Discourses. He teaches his students that prosoche is necessary for an ethical life and that even less evidently critical activities can be conducted with prosoche, such as singing or playing. Its implementations, indeed, are infinite. Is there some aspect of life that Prosoche does not apply to? 'The preservation of prosoche is an integral aspect of Stoicism.

In Stoicism, the meaning of developing a centered mind is reminiscent of the Buddha's assertion in the Dhammapada that not a father, not a mother, can help us better as much as a well-directed mind. It is inherently curious that something so close to mindfulness was key to what it took to be a Stoic.

'Prosoche' is concerned with fostering the potential for daily circumstances to apply core ethical precepts. The most critical one was to make sure that you rely on what you can do, not on what you cannot manage. And more specifically, in ways that suit a benevolent social being, concentrate on doing what you can manage. As long as the first factor is concerned, a crucial question that anyone who practices Stoic mindfulness would ask themselves will then be, "Where do I" put myself "in this situation?" Do I put myself in something that I cannot control, or do I put myself in something that I can control? If you 'put yourself' in the approval of your boss, something that is beyond your influence, so when she agrees, you will be content and deflated when she does not.

If you 'put yourself' in the approval of your boss, something that is beyond your influence, so when she agrees, you will be content and deflated when she does not. As a Stoic, you would treat the situation differently, thinking, what is up to me in this scenario? For e.g.,' up to you' will be to concentrate on doing my job well and calmly. Maintaining your relationship with your boss as much as possible from your side will also be "up to you." But other than that, there is nothing "up to you."

If you find that your emotions are 'investing' themselves in something you cannot manage, Epictetus told his pupils, remember to say to yourself, that is nothing to do with you. Only focus your attention on what you can do and do it well.

Let's have some ways to fulfill your spirit with stoic mindfulness.

- **Abandon Your Vanity**

    The first step to getting in touch with yourself is to be true to yourself. Shed the false beliefs about your being. Know who you are and have no shame of accepting it to flourish.

    Epictetus was born a slave; he lived in Rome, was then exiled, and spent the remainder of his time in Greece. He said it is difficult for a person to understand what he already feels he knows.

    If you want to follow the philosophy and, thus, any matter of interest to you, before you start, you must throw away conceit and unnecessary pride. Be willing to understand, be willing to set your pride behind ad to be willing to listen to the wisdom of others, and accept the pleasure of ignorance to understand, flourish, and create.

There is a Socratic irony, like "I know I do not know nothing."

The definition of modesty is the feeling or mentality that makes you better than anyone or possessing a lack of pride that you have no special value. Humility seems like a bad trait at first sight, more like a sign of vulnerability rather than power. In fact, humility is a form of modesty that, as an individual, a contender, and a leader, will get you very far in your life. Let's take another way at it. An individual is arrogant who lacks modesty. It is a person who just cares about himself and sees himself as better and better than others. As they do not understand their shortcomings, there is no place for an arrogant person to better themselves. An individual who is not humble does not have a mentality for progress. The world's greatest teachers continue to make mistakes. The best teacher in the world also has plenty to learn about the world, and as not only a trainer but also a pupil, they should always perform their duties. You would never be able to achieve your full potential if you do not grab the opportunity to see your own flaws. Life is a never-ending road of development and learning. Pride deprives a person of their capacity to accomplish.

For self-improvement, modesty is an asset. You consider the aspects of your life that require attention while leading a modest life. If your teacher proposes to adjust a method to help your ring results, you need to understand that your current technique might not be ideally tailored to your goals. That comes with letting the preconceived concepts go and trusting the teacher. You should allow these experiences to fuel your development and learning only with modesty and emotional intelligence.

- **Shorten Your Expectations**

Be mindful of the world. Be able to distinguish what is achievable and what is not. Most of us are torn by the duality between what is happening in our heads and what is really happening around us.

All of us have such assumptions that things can go in a particular direction. It carries set expectations for some of us that our relationships should be just as we have imagined: ideal spouse, relatives, children, and friends. For some, it is the hope that by now we should have it all worked out, that our careers should follow a carefully planned path, or that any special occasion should live up to the hype: birthday, engagement, or holiday abroad.

The problem with this line of reasoning is that higher aspirations are not equal to higher satisfaction, appreciation, or success ratings. In comparison, projecting set goals is in profound contrast to life-defining impermanence and uncertainty. To deny the fabric of life is to demand things to go towards a predetermined direction. No matter how hard you try, you will not and cannot erase all the confusion from your life.

There is no such thing as the way it should be, in fact. It is all in a state of continuous motion. The more you try to eradicate doubt and complexity from life, the narrower your comfort zone's confines get. True ease is discovered by accepting pain, not defending oneself from uncertainty, and this is the comfort paradox. The broader the spectrum of future situations you have prepared yourself to contend with, the better things can work out.

It is not that expectations are risky necessarily. Yet they become precisely that as we rely on a particular result beyond what the Stoics viewed as our 'reasoned decision,' one about which we have little to no power. Positive visualization is not so much a tactic as it is a blueprint for disappointment, putting hopes sky-high and focusing solely on the best-case situation. You will end up ruined sooner or later by someone outside your influence.

Expectations leave you weak, static, and reactive outside of your rational decision. It is limiting and inefficient to spend your scarce resources on attempting to control any variable and going from A to B as you have imagined it in your mind. It restricts what you are going to do, what you can do, and the person you are going to be.

And who is invincible then? The one that will not be distracted by anything beyond their reasoned choice.

A much more powerful strategy provided by the Stoics is pessimistic visualization, considering the spectrum of future effects, even the adverse and worst-case. The best minds do not sit around dreaming about an alternative, fanciful reality where everything plays out according to schedule. To navigate unavoidable hurdles and turn them to their benefit, they build resourcefulness.

The only worth-holding assumption is that you take advantage of chances to behave in compliance with your own beliefs and ideals. You should hope, regardless of present conditions or challenges, to harness your own resourcefulness and endurance to strengthen yourself. Build a momentum of your own.

It all boils down to the outlook. Prepare yourself to manage a variety of possible consequences, gain trust in that capacity, and restrict your assumptions beyond your reasoned preference. You rob failures and external events of their ability to catch you off balance and dictate your life as you follow this attitude.

Resilience rewards truth. It blinds you to anything except the one-track, imagined road you've expected by projecting predetermined goals of life. The mediation between truth and desires is at the base of both of these Stoic teachings.

Recognizing this inner war helps you to close the divide and continue to cultivate the mindfulness, discipline, and endurance it requires to make your own positive change. Otherwise, the only life you have is at risk of being detached and unhappy.

- **Moderation Approach**

    Being mindful requires you to understand the correct ratio of everything you do. Know the limits. Know the boundaries.

    As a society, we are proud of being extremes. We flaunt how we manage a few hours of sleep, how insatiable we are in our professions, and how luxurious our lives are due to an abundance of expensive goods. But the concern is that we still run the risk of taking our virtues too far as we strive to extremes, which crumble into their reverse, crushing character defects.

    Qualities and virtues are not just something you do or something you do not have. Varying degrees of severity exist. In this case, a dualistic mindset proves risky when two categories struggle to capture the complexity that distinguishes existence. The tendency to label personal attributes as positive or poor and no in-between should be ignored.

Instead, using Aristotle's 'golden mean,' it is much more reliable to frame virtues in the sense of a continuum, which explains that the range of goodness is squarely located in the center, between abundance and deficiency. Seneca gives a related viewpoint as he observes that so-called pleasures, when they go past a certain point, are actually punishments.

The premise is that we see those on one end of the continuum who neglect a certain attribute and view it as a defect. Yet virtues are just as prominent indicators of failure in their abundance. In fact, you can be too competitive (insatiable), too caring (co-dependent), and too disciplined (repressed). In the delicate spectrum of virtue, only those that represent balance can identify this golden mean, shield themselves from the downside of the extremes, and create an equilibrium.

Let me help you understand:

1. **Between Being Lazy and Being Insatiable Lies Ambition:** Laziness is an enemy that is evident and a symptom of vulnerability. But in the other direction, the continuum extends further than ambition. A virtue is a measured ambition. It is important to have ambitions, goals, and a purpose towards which you are working. Yet we cross into the domain of insatiability when taken too far.

   This is where we burn out, unable to reconcile with the moment, and understand what we have in our lives already. Insatiability, in equal relation to laziness, is a defect. Retaining personal well-being becomes an impossible challenge without moderation of our goals.

2. **Between Being Fragile and Being Depleted Lies Endurance:** Among top performers, endurance is a common virtue. It is interchangeable with emotional and physical stamina in this sense. Many who lack the stamina to conquer the challenges of life are weak and will not exhibit the persistence necessary to set themselves apart. On the other hand, though, there is a breaking point, utter fatigue, where you have nothing to offer.

   Building resilience is critical. But know the breaking point in the training and guard yourself against burnout. You have got a restricted amount of energy. Only things that fall in line with your professional goals and priorities should be delegated with that energy. Do not crash into the dirt yourself.

3. **Between Being Cold and Being Co-Dependent Lies Empathy:** Empathy is more advantageous than indifference or coldness. The stronger and healthier your relationships will be, the more you will be able to handle specific circumstances if you are in tune with those around you. If left unchecked, though, empathy will contribute to codependence and derive your self-worth from satisfying others' emotional needs while neglecting your own.

   Holding these extremes in mind is necessary so that you can use them as a checkpoint to work within the spectrum of morality. Check yourself, but still, make an attempt to distance yourself from such relationships if you find yourself in circumstances where people misuse your empathetic disposition.

- **Being Your Best Self**

Stoic Mindfulness is all about understanding yourself and then being the best possible version of yourself. Understand your flaws and do your best to polish your character.

Here are a few things which will help you be your best self:

1. **Finding Inspiration:** There is an explanation of why Marcus Aurelius' meditations begin with him, giving thanks to all those who played a part in his character's growth. Now, not all of us have the luxury of being surrounded socially by individuals who are a daily source of motivation for us. But fortunately, we live in a period where, at our fingertips, the wisdom of the best people ever to live is available. All we have to do is to look for them and learn all about what it means to live with justice, with intent, with strength, with bravery, and with joy.

2. **Reading:** The single biggest shortcut to learning about the persons we aspire to imitate is by learning to read. Perhaps it is the shortest road to changing oneself. Particularly today, where access to almost all of the world's information is available at our fingertips, some of it dating back to potentially millions of years before our creation. It acts as a reminder of our own ephemeral nature and that it is so important not to waste all of the short time on this planet that we have.

3. **Being Virtuous:** The Stoics concluded that our desire to become our best self lies in direct relation to how much the four main foundations of

virtue are followed—wisdom, boldness, justice, and temperance. We should be assured that no matter what happens, we can be prepared to benefit from anything that happens to us by making the acquisition of knowledge one of our key goals in a given year. We will face each of these scenarios with determination and never give up by exercising bravery, no matter how challenging they can appear. We will protect ourselves from giving into excess by exercising temperance and never let our feelings get the best of us when it is most necessary. And we will know from practicing justice that no matter what the result of our cases is, we really wanted to do the right thing.

4. **Saving Time:** The remorse that accumulates as the years go on is one of the hardest things about not sticking to our resolutions. Then we get to the end of our lives and remember how much time we have lost, how much time we have been losing in our own ways. All the times we give in to frustration when it was within our control not to, and how much this has a negative effect on our lives, we know.

5. **Building Resilience:** The only big determinant of our fate lies in how we react to what happens to us. Not in the stuff itself. Think of the ones you most respect, those who have faced immense challenges and made them happier and stronger. Do not let your first instinct be to get off the path if anything negative occurs. Let this be a chance to learn and to bring out of yourself the brightest. The more you overcome adversity, the better you become.

6. **Being Practical:** The goal of learning Stoic philosophy is to enrich the way we live our lives with any other facet. Stoicism is probably the most realistic of all philosophies, after all. It is not about arguing whether

there is such a thing as free will or other complex universe philosophies, but about encouraging us to transcend negative feelings and act on what should be achieved. It is meant to keep us calm under pressure and to concentrate on our values. But there is no point in reading the letters of Seneca if we are not going to add them to our own lives immediately. Marcus Aurelius noted in the above quotation that in order to become the best version of ourselves, there just are not that many things we have to practice. It is possible to understand these things through thought, but can completely comprehend them through experience. When you do exactly that in the most stressful circumstances, you do not fully understand the strength of letting go of your rage. When you see how much peace it would offer you to do so. All of this makes you more and more powerful and ready to survive the future challenges to which we will eventually be exposed.

- **Being Sincere**

As described above, be mindful of what you can control and what you cannot. Obsessing over things that are not in your control will only leave you hurt. Be sincere in what you do, and do not be greedy about the results.

For example, there is an example of a performer with stage-fright, and it is provided by Epictetus. He said to himself when he saw a man in anxiety, what could this fellow want? For if he did not want anything outside his grasp, how could he be anxious? That is why he displays little discomfort when performing on his own but does so as he reaches the theatre, even though he has a wonderful voice. Since he does not only want to sing well but to win applause as well, and that is no longer in his influence. Oh, why is that? Why he actually does not know what an audience is, or the crowd's applause. That is why he trembles and becomes pale. The singer's desire is to want the audience to cheer him.

When he does, he leaves all puffed up. By comparison, the Stoic singer insists solely on the success of his craft and does that well. If the audience applauds, he will be pleased, but that has never been the point of his singing. For making a presentation or voice, the same may happen. The irony, of course, is that the one who insists on his artwork, on being in the field, is more likely to do his or her job well and to win the crowd's applause. In brief, a simple practice of Stoic mindfulness may be to question yourself during the day at numerous points: why am I putting myself in this situation?

These are the few ways you can truly live your life to the most with stoic mindfulness.

Chapter 7 – Turn Yourself into a Better Person

My advice to you, as this is the last chapter of the book, is to maintain your focus on being a better person, and you can do that through Stoicism. We have got countless things to attend to on a daily basis. We have got emails to reply to and calls to make. There are meetings. The people we met yesterday are waiting for a response or a decision we promised we would make. Facebook beckons. And so do our dreams and our aspirations.

And still, no matter how many directions we find ourselves in, it is fair to say that Marcus Aurelius was under much greater stress. Make no mistake: a calm, peaceful place was not the ancient world. Crises and distractions, rumors, and optimistic goal-setting filled it, too. In the past, all the temptations we faced now have their analogies, plus situations were scarier, deadlier, and precarious.

Let's discuss the stoic approach to staying focused.

7.1 Sharpen Your Focus – The Stoic Way

We should listen to the order that Marcus gave himself when he was struggling to stay focused after one of those trying days. He said that focus on doing what is in front of you with strictly and with sincere seriousness, tenderly, happily, with justice.

And he was not just chiding himself for doing something unthinkable. There was a process, he said, for this concentration. Do it all as if it was the last thing you did in your life. That is Memento Mori's power. The key, Marcus said, was not to let your impulses override your mind and offer a clear reason to yourself. Aimlessness is a diversion enabler.

You have got the ability to concentration like a Roman. You should handle everything correctly. And you can, most importantly. Because that might well be the last act of your life that you do. Below are a few stoic ways to deal with lack of concentration towards your goals in life:

- **Doing Less**

    Do less if you want tranquility. Do what is crucial. Do less and do it well. Since it is not important to any of what we do or say. You would get more tranquility if you can remove it. But we still need to eliminate unnecessary expectations in order to eliminate the behavior taken.

    We are so focused now on doing more things that we are losing sight of what is really important. What is worst, we are trying to achieve everything that is impractical, and we wind up going nowhere. Our to-do list is so big that we actually get off on hitting it all off.

    For this purpose, Pareto's 80/20 theory can be used. The aim is to commit resources to the most relevant 2-3 activities that are expected to earn us higher returns.

    So, look at your work list and ask yourself these questions:

    1. What is the optimal result if I complete this assignment? This will help you in thinking about the returns.
    2. How can I automate this task? It will help you concentrate your resources on items that really need your energy, leaving the rest to computers.

3. How can this assignment benefit me or anyone else? It will help you pull items out that are not likely to benefit anyone.

It is excellent to see more work get done. But, it is quite possible that the quality of the job will also be poor. Instead, consider the fact that we have a limited span of focus and reflect on sorting out two-three of the day's most important things and devoting the undivided attention to completing them.

- **Identify Control**

The key challenge in life is precisely is to classify and differentiate problems so that you can reassure yourself plainly that they are external, not under your influence, and that they have to do with the decision that you really influence. Where do you look for the good and for bad, then? Not to uncontrollable externals, but to the decisions that are your own inside you.

You would have found something if you visualized the process of a task — sometimes, not every stage of the process is within your influence. Working alongside others is a required skill in the new workplace. And it makes sense, to some degree, why we cannot do everything on our own.

Now, although partnering with others is fantastic for the organization's general benefit, it could leave us a little stuck on our road to productivity.

So, what can be done when we work for teams, and not everything is in our control? We can discriminate easily between actions that are in our hands and actions that are not.

The Stoics accepted the fact that not everything is beyond our influence in our lives. And therefore, it is not only irrational to get angry over these uncontrollable actions, but it can also drive us crazy. There will be no amount of complaining about your co-worker that will help them do their work. The fact of the matter is — we cannot influence the decisions and actions of other people.

Yet, we are able to monitor our job completely. To know that a certain part of the process is under our power, we should get clarification and leave the rest to others. And do our jobs.

- **Visualizing the Process**

Often, when we begin working on something, we fail to think about the process clearly. We only start with aspirations that are unreasonable. And this absence of clarification contributes to procrastination.

A blueprint for disaster that is all it is.

Applying logic to the tasks we do will mean gradually breaking down each task into discrete phases from the beginning until the process is visualized at the end. This will help us better identify how projects pass from one point to another and whether there are any obvious bottlenecks in the process, as well. This exercise will allow us to see the appropriate individual steps, allowing us a more practical understanding of what we can do with a hundred percent concentration today.

Mind Maps are valuable guides that will help us break down the method and see clearly the steps taken to execute a mission.

So, break down the three most significant activities for the day that you intend to achieve. Ask yourself about the desired outcome and, step by step, list the procedure. Focus then, with undivided attention, on one move at a time.

That is a formula for deep work.

Additionally, you will find that every single move is necessary once you disintegrate something into its individual pieces. In fact, however, work does not have a character. There is no "grunt work' in existence. There is a purpose behind every step that leads to something bigger.

- **Defining Success**

We are all well mindful of the fact that success is reliant on many factors. Some, in our power, whereas others, not quite. Our commitment is included under our total command, while external factors include items such as luck and the efforts of other individuals (in the case of a team task). And still, despite realizing this, failure at anything drives us off.

To the Stoics, pleasure meant doing their work. And the same philosophy, to some degree, may be attributed to success. Success is not meant to be whether or not we have done anything. Instead, the amount of work we put into a project should be determined by it. It needs to be the degree to which we have done our work.

Not only does this perception take complete hold over us, but it also allows us to focus when things do not turn out. And if there is anything we believe about reflection, it is that it makes us smarter.

So, calculate your success by your commitment the next time you focus on something. You have won, as long as you put your 100 percent into it. That is success. The results are external. Your efforts are internal.

By following the above four methods to sharpen your focus, you can make yourself more successful. Below we will discuss the three aspects of stoic philosophy to live a life of harmony and bliss.

7.2 Employ Disciplines of Stoicism – Key to a Harmonious Life

A very detailed study of the meditations of Marcus Aurelius called The Inner Citadel was published by the French intellectual Pierre Hadot, in which he discusses the Three Disciplines in-depth, using them as a basis for his exposition. If we pursue the reading of Hadot, it simply gives a fairly straightforward and basic model for interpreting Stoicism's teachings. Traditionally, the way of Stoic philosophy was described as living according to nature or living harmoniously, and Hadot implies that all three disciplines are built to help us live in peace in various ways and that they join together to provide the secret of a harmonious and a serene way of life, practical philosophy as the discipline of living wisely. Here are the three stoic disciplines:

- **The Discipline of Assent**

    The discipline of "assent", according to Hadot, is the extension of the Stoic metaphysical subject of "logic" to everyday life. In reality, stoic "logic" contains components of what we would now label "epistemology." or "psychology." According to this view, the discipline of the agreement is the virtue of living as human beings in harmony with our own intrinsic essence, which entails living with both our thoughts and words with conformity with reason and truthfulness. It is tempting to see this practice as especially synonymous with "wisdom" or truthfulness as the cardinal Stoic virtue. Hadot calls the "inner citadel" the aim of this discipline because it requires constant knowledge of the actual self, the part of the mind responsible for reasoning and behavior, the chief good of life, where our independence and morality remain. According to the study of Hadot, while the Stoics usually refer to "judgment," they are mainly interested in tracking and analyzing their own implied value judgments. This forms the foundation of our acts, impulses, and feelings, in particular the irrational urges and vices that the Stoics were seeking to resolve. Stoics are to note the early-warning signals of disturbing or unhealthy impressions by constantly observing their judgments and taking a step back from them, maintaining their "assent" or consent, rather than getting "carried away" into unreasonable and unhealthy passions and vices. This prosochê, or "attention," is named by the Stoics to the governing faculties of the mind, to our decisions and acts.

- **The Discipline of Action**

According to Hadot, the action discipline "hormê", which means the beginning or original" impulse "to action) is the implementation of the Stoic metaphysical subject of" ethics "to everyday life. Stoic "ethics" require the concept of positive, evil, and indifferent things. The goal of life is often dealt with as "happiness" or satisfaction (eudaimonia). It requires the concept (righteousness, wisdom, self-discipline, and bravery) of the cardinal Stoic virtues. According to the fundamental doctrine of Stoicism, for good living and satisfaction, goodness is the only true good and necessary in itself. Stoic ethics also include the vices, resisting morality, and the "passions" that are unreasonable and pathological, defined as craving, anxiety, physical distress, and pathological or deceptive pleasures. According to Hadot, the discipline of behavior is basically the practice of living in peace with all humanity, which implies benevolently wishing all humanity to prosper and fulfill the purpose of life with satisfaction. Nevertheless, since the well-being of other persons is beyond our immediate jurisdiction, we must still wish them well in compliance with the Stoic "reserve clause" (hupexairesis), which literally implies inserting the caveat: "Fate allowing" or "God willing." This is one way in which robust behavior with emotional recognition is reconciled by the spiritual approach towards life. In other terms, Stoics do their best to behave with virtue while acknowledging in a rather distant way, whether success or loss, the product of their acts. In addition, Stoics would function on the basis of their objective estimation on which external consequences should necessarily be desired. Marcus Aurelius thus seems to refer to three clauses which Stoics should be constantly mindful of adding to, all their actions the following:

1. A reserve clause (hupexairesis)

2. Collective good (koinônikai)

3. Sensitivity to value (kat' axian)

It is tempting to see this discipline as specially related to the cardinal virtue of "justice," which the Stoics described as including equality and benevolence towards others. Hadot calls this discipline "action in the service of humanity" because, by a mechanism known as "appropriation" (oikeiosis) or expanding the circle of our inherent "self-love" to encompass all humanity, it means extending the same natural affection or concern that we are born experiencing for our own bodies and physical well-being to include the mental and physical well-being of all mankind.

- **The Discipline of Desire**

The discipline of "desire" (orexis) is, according to Hadot, the application of the Stoic metaphysical subject of "physics" to everyday life, which involves the Stoic study of cosmology, natural philosophy, and theology. According to this view, the discipline of desire is a practice of living in accordance with the essence of the world as a whole, or with Zeus or Deity in the language of Stoic theology. This includes taking a "philosophical approach" as necessary and natural for existence and recognition of our destiny. The cardinal virtues synonymous with self-control over excessive desires, which are "courage" or endurance in the face of fear and pain and "self-discipline" (temperance) or the capacity to renounce temptation and abstain from deceptive or harmful pleasures, are especially enticing to see this discipline as involving. Hadot names this discipline's goal "Amor fati," or the caring embrace of one's destiny. One of the most compelling passages from the Enchiridion sums up this discipline that does not look for events to happen as you like, but for events to happen as they do and your life will proceed serenely and smoothly. The Stoic soldier Cato of Utica famously marched through the deserts of Africa through the broken remains of the Republican army to make a dramatic last defense against the tyrant Julius Caesar, who attempted to topple the Republic and proclaim himself Rome's emperor. He became a Roman hero even after he lost the civil war, and the Stoics called him "the mighty Cato" because his will was absolutely unconquered-he ripped his own heart out with his bare hands instead of submitting to Caesar and being used for his propaganda by the tyrant. Centuries later, despite a crippling plague and numerous misfortunes beyond his grasp, the Stoic emperor Marcus Aurelius repeatedly led his depleted army into battle to protect Rome from invading barbarian hordes.

Regardless of the many challenges to conquest, he won. Rome would have been lost if he had failed.

These are three disciplines action, assent, and desire.

I have discussed the two factors which play into being your best self and living your best life in a serene manner. I would like to discuss two more aspects that play into living your life in the best possible way, and these are renouncing negative emotions and self-discipline.

7.3 Stop Fostering Negativity – Critical for a Positive Life

Stoic thought's objective is not to mitigate unpleasant emotions but to see the world as it is and foster virtue. Emotions matter because they hinder the universe from being viewed correctly. When we get caught up in them, it happens. When they move towards behaving without purpose, emotions count as bad.

The focus is not, from this viewpoint, on reducing negative emotions. The emphasis is on behaving with rationality and being committed to acting on our principles.

When one focuses one's mind on mitigating bad feelings, this dynamic will arise. Rumination may be driven by battling them. Rumination can give way to pessimistic thoughts. It continues the loop.

Imagine a pessimistic thought as a flame. A burning flame will not do any harm in an empty concrete parking lot. These flames are left on their own to die out or are quickly extinguished. In a locked space packed with combustible material, bring the blaze, and you have a possible tragedy on your side.

The fire would use any bit of flammable material in the space to burn hotter, longer, and stronger until it is quickly extinguished. .The single blaze left uninterrupted will become an uncontainable inferno that will burn until its flames have nothing left to feed on.

People feel a common scenario when they are a host to negativity. By the time it eventually runs its course, a person has been broken by all the rage, resentment, and blame from physical, emotional, and spiritual fatigue.

In a way, emotions are a tool. They are able to provide useful world knowledge and inspire us to behave well. When we get caught up in them and losing contact with reality, they get in the way. When we confuse feeling with how things are and when they influence us to behave in ways we would not reflectively support, feelings blind us.

The way to fix this is not to preclude bad thoughts from being encountered. We should embrace the bad emotions as they are. One may practice through typical stoic techniques, such as praemeditatio Malorum or by meditation,

Why does it matter? As the target distracts from what is really important, tension reduces negative emotions. Instead of staying out of one's mind and behaving with virtue, one's time can be expended battling toxic feelings. In comparison, working on reducing bad thoughts will make them worse.

I hope you have understood now how much negative emotions can put a strain on your life, and it is absolutely essential to break the negative cycle, so you do not faint running in circles from exhaustion. Let's move on to self-discipline.

7.4 Self-Discipline – Biggest Secret to a Fulfilling Life

Troubling moments make you feel as if the entire life is coming to a standstill. Life never fails to move and evolve. Time cures, and you are going to find yourself moving again, so you are going to have to do it in your own way. Difficulties are part of growth.

You can get better from a situation, but only if you have the right attitude. Some lessons may include: learning to let go of the past, being stronger, speaking more clearly, forgiving and rising, and putting faith in your gut. Life is a blessing; keep loving it, do not forget. We have little power over many of the external situations, but what we do have power over is the way we react. Existence is frail. Spend your time to enjoy life wisely. Life is intended to be experienced, to be felt and appreciated profoundly. Scientific analysis is demonstrating that it promotes cell development in the brain by taking on challenges. It encourages us to cope and to create resilience.

Discipline is the basic action, attitude, and ideology that holds a person in a routine and makes progress towards which he or she is following. Philosophy is not just about chatting or reading dense texts. It is something that people have used to accomplish their personal and professional accomplishments throughout history.

Our ego most frequently runs away from something that tells us of the fact that it is at odds with the cozy narrative we have made for ourselves. Any new pursuit is vital to its starting point. Stoicism doesn't make a difference. Stoicism is a practice we should use to become better friends, better in the profession, and better people overall. Without self-discipline, no personal progress, accomplishment, or goal can be realized. It is the most critical quality required for some sort of personal or technical excellence or excellent results to be attained. We also discover the hard way that external forces rule our universe. No phase takes place immediately, just as muscle building takes time, so self-discipline takes time to create. The more you practice and develop, the more you get stronger.

An integral feature of Stoic philosophy is self-discipline. Stoicism, not authoritarianism, is about self-discipline. We have actually no clue what other people are dealing with. The Stoics tell us because we have no idea what their inner world is like. We would not judge them if we did.

Through the mastery of our emotions, self-regulation begins. You cannot regulate what you do if you do not regulate what you say. Motivation keeps you moving; you keep rising with discipline. This is why we cannot let strangers decide whether or not anything is worth it. Within us is the secret to success.

These are the four aspects explained in Stoicism, which can lead you to be better as a human being.

I hope this book excited your minds about Stoicism, and you have grasped the fundamentals of this philosophy. The second part of this book is the practical version of this one. The detailed 30,000 words solely entail everyday practices and exercises for the modern stoics at home and also in the workplace so they can find real happiness. So if you want to live happily, which is something not very common and almost impossible in this chaotic world, you do need an understanding of Stoicism to help you achieve that. Stoicism teaches you that in reality, it is not the world around you, which is chaotic; it is our mind which is chaotic. Peace comes from within.

Conclusion

You have the authority to build the life that you desire. Learning how to become emotionally strong is an important ability that can help you get there. This book is a chance at life for people who lack emotional stability. The good news is that mental power is like a muscle: the more you use it, the better it gets. That would put an end to a continuous cycle of procrastinating your goals, big or small, and finally, bring the discipline to your life that would lead you to live a fulfilling life. You would not let others bring you down either by their words or actions. You would not stop believing in yourself, and you will never be a victim of circumstance. You would stand strong in the face of adversities. You would finally understand that you have control over your reactions to external factors, and that is a game-changer.

Emotional stability and all the good things in life come with stoicism. Stoicism is an ancient philosophy initially put forward by a rich merchant, Zeno of Citium, around 301 BC. The most prominent teaching of stoicism is to focus on the inside to prepare a sensible response to the outside and not letting the external events have control over your life. Important figures like Walt Whitman, George Washington, Frederick the Great, Adam Smith, and many more have been found to study, admire, and follow stoicism.

The three prominent teachers of stoicism after Zeno were Seneca, Marcus Aurelius, and Epictetus. One was a roman emperor, and the other was a slave. This shows the diversity of the application of this philosophy. All three of them made significant contributions to the way of life that is stoicism. Most of the teachings of Seneca come in the form of letters. He wrote a collection of essays on diverse, realistic matters like adversity, mortality, frustration, tranquility, leisure, and happiness. Marcus wrote a book Meditations that is the authoritative book on personal integrity, self-discipline, modesty, power, and self-actualization. Epictetus wrote a handbook filled with stoic maxims and values, and there is a collection of discourses as an interaction between him and his students on topics like friendship, sickness, anxiety, hunger, tranquility, and why other people need not be upset with each other.

The first chapter serves an introductory purpose of the stoic philosophy. Stoicism has been manipulated as the emotionless philosophy of the ancient period, but what it truly is a powerful tool to bring your emotions and actions in a well-defined harmony. It got its name from Stoa Poikilê, a place for Zeno and his students to get together and celebrate the teachings of stoicism. There are four virtues in stoicism, namely justice, courage, temperance, and wisdom. These virtues are the fundamentals of the stoic philosophy, and there is still to date nothing more valuable in life than these four values, and there will never be anything more valuable too.

Stoicism stands on many core-beliefs like agreement with nature, focusing on the controllable, living by virtue, understanding the difference between good, bad and indifferent, taking action, loving the undesired, practicing misfortune, making opportunities, mindfulness, and many more.

The second chapter encompasses the journey of stoicism and covers the classical stoic period divided into three time zones. Stoicism has found a significant place among the modern generation as it revived because of three major reasons like the failure of social structures, massive information accessibility, and the undeniable nature of its advice. People who have made big names in the modern-day like Bill Gates, Elon Musk, Pete Carroll, and Warren Buffett, all owe their success to stoicism. The ancient philosophy offers solutions to many modern-day problems.

The third chapter deals with stoic practices that can still be applicable in the modern-day like stoic acceptance, time-saving, going beyond pleasure, embracing your distress, and strict honesty.

Chapter four is dedicated to building emotional resilience through practices like stoic meditation, avoiding impossible hope, accepting fate, Momento Mori (reminding yourself of death), Premeditatio Malorum (contemplating on the worst that could happen), accepting difficulties, responding to and turning hardships into opportunities for growth and eradicating ego.

Chapter five is comprised of dealing with anger, fear, greed, trauma, and stress in accordance with the stoic teachings like distinguishing pain from suffering, creating a gratitude list, understanding that you are not perfect, and many more.

The sixth chapter includes ways to nurture stoic mindfulness like abandoning vanity, shortening expectations, acquiring a moderate approach, and being your best self by finding inspiration, being sincere, being virtuous, and building resilience.

The final chapter of this book deals with being the best version of yourself. It can be done by sharpening your focus, acquiring the three disciplines of stoicism, i.e., action, assent, and desire, renouncing negative emotions, and maintaining self-discipline.

If there is one thing that I want you to take away from my book is to live in accordance with nature. If you are mindful of yourself, you will be able to better control how you respond to the happenings around you.

The second part of this book is fully equipped with daily routine exercises and practices. This book would not be just applicable in your personal life but also in your workplace so you can be happy in the truest sense. It is a detailed book of 30,000 solely devoted to the practical use of stoicism. Make sure you check it out as it can offer you the secrets of a peaceful and fulfilling life, which is getting harder and harder to achieve in the modern world.

How to Practice Stoicism

Lead the Stoic way of Life to Master the Art of Living, Emotional Resilience & Perseverance - Make your everyday Modern life Calm, Confident & Positive

Written By

Marcus Epictetus

Introduction

Stoicism was formulated to help people live the best possible lives and become the best versions of themselves. It is a philosophy of life that maximizes your positive emotions, minimizes the negative emotions, and helps people lead a contented life. At any point, at different stages of life, it provides a practical framework to live well. It gives a clear distinction between things that are truly important and things that should not bother you at all. Stoicism provides practical ways and strategies to lead a valuable life. It was designed to be actionable, understandable, and useful individuals.

Practicing Stoicism does not require mastering a new philosophy. Instead, it provides an immediate, practical, and useful way to achieve tranquility and improve your character's strengths. The philosophy of Stoicism has developed over time. It has shifted its focus from physics and logic to psychological goals like well-being and tranquility.

The practices of Stoicism are not just about learning some interesting ideas. They should also be practiced each day of your life. Most people are aware of the philosophy of Stoicism. They also try to become a stoic in routine life, but they do not know how to practice Stoicism in the right way. Over time, people have little patience and tolerance for theoretical contemplation. They want to focus on the real-world application where they look for an answer to take action.

Stoicism is about getting out and live by the theory. This is the only way to build the righteous and meaningful life. Stoics believe in the moral action. To live in peace, you have to live morally. Stoicism acknowledges that we cannot control everything that comes our way or whatever happens in our life. So, worrying about those things that cannot be controlled is totally unproductive and irrational if your goal is to achieve tranquility.

It is crucial to remind yourself daily to differentiate what is in control and what is beyond your control. Stoicism practically teaches you to let go of uncontrollable events and do not waste your energy over them. Instead, put that energy to think of a creative solution. Placing focus on the solutions rather than problems and issues themselves is the key to successfully implementing this philosophy. Stoicism teaches that controlling the events rather than controlling ourselves will cause us a great harm. Attempts to control this world will lead to failure and disappointment, but controlling oneself will never cause disappointment.

This book includes the full day routine of stoic practices with precise directions so that everyone can easily follow this. This book includes practices stated by Marcus Aurelius. By reading and following the practices given in this book, you will care less about what people think. You will be more cautious whenever you think of wasting your time. You will always remember what is in your control so that you can save yourself from distractions.

Seeing the world in the light of Stoicism philosophy makes us believe that whatever happens in any part of the world and to a distant individual, is crucial to our lives. It fosters and builds our empathy towards each other. It builds a strong social justice for our self-interest. The justice, then, pertains to every member of the society. It promotes harmony. Stoicism also recognizes equality, which is compulsory if we all want to attain the true fulfillment and live rightly. It all starts with our own actions.

Think and act in the ways that emphasize similarities and also increases our quest for justice and compassion. The climate change issue, for example, requires us to develop these qualities and be united in this. It is apparent that the society we are living in, is moving fast in the direction of detachment - focusing on divergent political perspectives, religious and racial differences, and our different lifestyle choices.

Stoicism provides this modern world with a way to combat and work against this fractured trend. It reflects a need to restore fairness and simplicity to current human ethics codes. In this situation, going back to the ancient school and philosophy of thought is the sensible step in moving forward. As Marcus Aurelius suggests to keep moving on a road cheerfully, making efficient use of whatever is on hand and what looks right at that moment. This approach has worked in the past. It will work now.

Most of us see Stoicism as the need for the 21st century. Many people fondly read Epictetus, Marcus Aurelius, and Seneca, who are the prominent stoic teachers. Stoicism's success in modern times resides in its practicability and timelessness. By practicing Stoic guidelines, anyone can achieve the tangible improvements and tranquility in every aspect of life.

The playwright and political counselor, Seneca was a philosopher and a follower of the philosophy of Stoicism. The best thing about him was that he wrote many readable and exciting things. Seneca wrote an exciting collection of essays that dealt with realistic problems, mortality, adversity, and frustration. He also wrote about leisure, tranquility, and happiness. His work also includes a variety of natural science topics like thunder and lightning, rivers, comets, and earthquakes.

The Roman Emperor Marcus Aurelius worked not just through the language or metaphysical doctrines but inspired through his way of living. He was better than most of the ancient influencers. Marcus' "Meditations" is one of his best works. It is about the personal perspectives and views in counseling himself on how to make a good life. It is one of the best and authoritative books on self-discipline, personal integrity, modesty, self-actualization, and power.

Epictetus was born in slavery. His book Enchiridion, a small textbook or a handbook, would be an ideal starting point for Epictetus. It offers brief Stoic maxims and values, and it is the introduction of Epictetus. Koine Greek is a series of personal but complicated conversations where Epictetus attempted to help and guide his students. He taught them about the Stoic's intellectual life and ways to live it. He addresses a variety of subjects, from anxiety to hunger, from friendship to sickness, how tranquility can be achieved and sustained in the long term, and why other people need not to be upset with one another.

This compelling and highly actionable guide will show you how to deal with whatever life throws at you and live up to your best self. It will guide you how you can get on with life itself effectively. It is not very common that everything valuable and meaningful to us goes exactly the way we want it to, and that is life. You have to deal with it. Now it is your choice; you want to do that either feeling helpless or feeling empowered.

This book has been written for you and it will act as your mentor in achieving self-control, self-resilience, and calmness. By following the practices discussed in the book, you will find the way to calmness, resilience & self-control that you will need to live well.

Continue reading this book if you simply wish to become the best possible version of yourself and change your perception of life and become a focused person with positivity.

Chapter 1: Full Day Stoic Routine

Modern life being extremely eventful and demanding creates problematic situations. The excitement, anxiousness, and a lot of other factors distract us and do not let us focus on ourselves. We need to live in the present and feel the moment. It might happen that you learn Stoicism and adopt its philosophy about life, but life will take over again. You might forget what you have learned. Tick to the principles of Stoicism, and you will be able to deal with any situation as it arises.

In this chapter, you will know how you can make a conscious effort to cement your life's philosophy. In this way, you will always have an effective response to whatever you will face every day. This guide will help you outline a Stoic routine for the whole day. It will hopefully give you a lot of clarity in life. Take baby step if you want to, and feel free in picking and choosing the practical steps towards your Stoicism journey.

1.1 Prepare Yourself for the day

As you are about to start the day, there might be many thoughts wandering in the head about dealing with your day in the coming 24 hours. Follow Marcus Aurelius' footsteps, and write a journal to get yourself better prepared. It does not need to have any specific technique, just put out your thoughts and clear your head.

Meditation

Stoicism is synonymous with stillness and meditation. The main idea is to gather your thoughts and be still. Ancient Stoicism has highlighted it, and it is equally effective even today. You can meditate in a lot of ways. Find the one that best suits you and your lifestyle. Morning meditation before breakfast works really well.

Think about your day ahead. Go through your plans, and sit motionless for about five minutes. Imagine a waterfall or any calm visual. It should take about almost ten minutes. This mundane act will become a habit, and it will prove to be a life-changing experience. It will help you approach your day with more determination and poise. It will reduce your stress levels.

According to Marcus Aurelius, our thoughts shape our lives. The mediation he recommends does not necessarily be zen or Buddhist meditation. Most people think it is all about that method. Meditation does not need to be just limited to sit down and focus on the breath. Meditation can be putting the focus on any thought, situation, or task.

Any form of meditation on a daily basis will help in controlling your anxiety. It will increase self-awareness and also your ability to focus and learn fast. Daily meditation helps promote mindfulness and awareness of your current situation and existence. It will all allow you to make small changes in your daily routine. It will let you live the way you want to live on this planet and give you a personal identity.

Avoid Social Media and News

Checking social media and scrolling through the latest news is tempting. It will take away your peace. You should save your precious time by avoiding these unproductive actions. You can achieve it with self-discipline. If you are successful in building this habit and consume less time on the content on social media that has been designed to distract you from your life, you will soon start to build a positive outlook while beginning your day.

Go Out for a Walk

Be in the open air for some time and go out for a walk. It will refresh you and raise your spirits. Take a family member, friend, or your dog with you. Go alone if you prefer that way. Appreciate the stillness and peace. It is a perfect end of the preparation for your day ahead.

1.2 Morning Routine

Every morning Marcus Aurelius used to remind himself what he needed to contribute to this world. That is where the real well-defined habits come to existence. During the period of the Roman Empire, his routine helped him in raising his productivity and self-control. The morning routine he had consisted of breakfast, self-reflection, and journaling. He used to plan his day and write about all potential struggles.

A well-managed morning routine, according to Stoic habits, is one of the effective ways to change your life. It may take some time to enable you identify the right morning habits, but once adopted, these habits will become major pillars of your life to have a truly successful day.

Your morning routine may include a shower, a meditation routine, a healthy breakfast, a walk, a reading ritual, and journaling. These habits will decide how your day would be like. You will notice that failing to fulfill these morning rituals will make you less productive. You might also feel unsatisfied without them.

Get Out of Bed

At dawn, if you feel trouble in waking up, remind yourself that you have work to do. There is nothing to complain about. You need to do what you have to do to contribute something to this world. This is what you were created for. Staying under the warm blankets is not something you were born for.

To do something, first, you need to get out of the bed, getting away from your clumsiness. Lying there will add nothing to the productivity of your day. It is the moment when the only obstacle is nothing else but yourself. It is not so hard to overcome it. After getting up, don't consider making your bed a trivial thing. That is also a big achievement.

Take a Shower

While people might not like a cold water shower each morning, it is worth practicing as it reduces your unnecessary dependence on being comfortable all the time. It tells you about your resilience level. There are many health benefits attached to it.

Dress Up

There is absolutely no need to become extravagant while choosing your clothing. When you feel content even with less, consider yourself on the right path.

Physical Exercise

The appearance should not be the end goal of physical exercise. The appearance comes in the end when we talk about its benefits. To put the unnecessary focus on physical appearance lead to vanity and narcissism. Exercise helps in mental clarity and general health. It prevents diseases and also alters the mental state and mood.

All these benefits of exercise are more crucial than six-pack appearance. It should be part of everyone's life. Start from less, then build it stronger by adding tough exercises like push-ups, etc. You should always do something each day to get your heartbeat working on letting your body sweat.

Eating breakfast

You should eat inexpensive food. Choose food that is easily available and healthy. Leaving unhealthy and fancy meals is one of the most effective ways to achieve self-control. It will benefit your health in the long-term.

1.3 Evening Routine

Every capability and habit grow with actions. If you really want to achieve something, make it your habit. If there is something you like to quit, also make a habit of shunning it. Stoicism focuses on routines and habits. Marcus used to have a morning ritual to start his day. Marcus's stepfather and mentor, Antoninus Pius, used to be so disciplined that he chose to limit his bathroom periods to save more time to do more productive things.

Without habits and rituals, you would never be able to do a challenging task. You would become the victim of resistance. It is true not just for this philosophy, but also about other professions and a desire to have a meaningful life. Habit and routine are the right ways. You cannot randomly improve. People do not do great jobs or make decisions just by accident. Routine will get you through life easily.

Socialize

Socialize as it is healthy for you. Nature has bound us to each other. It has taught us compatibility and mutual love. Hold everything together that is important to co-exist in this world. We all stem from one common source. We will fall apart if we do not support one another. So, go out once in a while and have a conversation with someone. Meet family and talk to even strangers.

Be Attentive

Consider everything as it is happening for the last time. In this way, you will become more focused and appreciate everything at the moment. Be present and attentive when you spend time with people. Put the phone away. It is not just about hearing, but actually listening to others.

Help Others

Remind yourself again and again that we all exist because of one another. If someone needs help, be ready, and help that person. Do not forget that you were in that position once, and someone did help you. Do not track your good deeds. Help but do not expect to get a reward in return.

Do not Indulge in Unnecessary Arguments

Arguments happen in our lives. We cannot control them. But we can control how we respond to them. You might be asked to give opinions on any topic. It is okay to put forward your perspective. But remember, there is always an option to have no opinion about things. Eliminate all the unnecessary distractions from life.

1.4 Be Stoic All Day Long

There is no specific time to act according to your Stoicism principles. Remember and practice them all day long. Keep them with yourself as something precious, to which you need to hold one. It might include looking for positivity in daily adverse situations, cutting out all the little and unproductive distractions, journaling, and doing something productive. You do not need one specific time to do all these things.

Look for Positivity

When we have to find positivity in negative situations, Stoicism can prove to be a life-saver. You have so much power over what you think and your mind. You do not try to control events. Realize your strength. Marcus Aurelius has always highlighted its importance. Learn to control your responses to negativity. When you accept this fact that you have no control over external events, you start to deal with them effectively.

Start to change your perceptions. Let go of despondence upon the external occurrences. For example, you recently lost a job. You are feeling sad. You immediately search for culprits so you could put the blame on them. You could play a blame game, or you could choose to respond with Stoic thinking. Identify your lesson from that particular experience, and then move on. Differentiate between the thing you can control and things you cannot. Never let the negativity consume you.

Cut out Distractions

You might be struggling with procrastination. Adopting Stoicism can prove to be a concentration booster. Stoics consciously avoid distractions and put their focus on their creativity. They are aware of the efforts that matter. Observe and know if the external matters distract you. According to Marcus Aurelius, make time to learn something that is worthwhile, and stop letting things pull you in many directions.

Direct your time and energy towards fruitful activities, and do not try to be master of everything all at once. Selectively using your time and resources advance your professional and personal quests.

Journaling

There is no specific time to write a journal. Write whenever you feel writing. Write about everything you want to put out in a notebook. Write about those small deeds that took you further in your life. Write about the arguments that proved to be futile in your relationships. Did this 30-minute client call contribute to the growth of my business? Journaling cuts out distractions. It utilizes your resources even more efficiently. It will improve your mindfulness and productivity in your everyday life.

Do Something Productive

We are given so much time to do great things in life. There are so many chances to spend our life well. Stoicism tells you to make the most out of what we have. It is a fact that life is temporary. It will not last forever. Stoicism helps us in appreciating each day of our life. So, use your time productively, and you will start to feel good. You will notice life is much longer than you think.

Each day can work in two ways. Either fill it with rewarding and productive activities or live it with distractions. When you spend your time well, you feel contented. You become satisfied that you have contributed your part. That is how you move forward. If you spend it without those productive activities, there is no denying the fact that you have wasted a golden opportunity.

1.5 Review Your Day

To review your day, one of the best ways is the journaling; you do that at other times in the day, but doing it in the evening will also give you more clarity. The Stoics saw its value in the evening too. The main purpose is to review what happened, what was your reaction, and how can you do better. It is a great way to make sure your day's efforts do not go in vain. They must be recorded to make improvements.

Keep watching over yourself, and record every day to review yourself. Marcus Aurelius used to do this with his Meditations. He uses to sit down to review his day to get personal clarity. He used to write to himself. It was not for the public. But it is still useful even today.

To make your mind flourished, you must improve and grow by asking yourself questions about the bad habit you put in today, the faults you made, and what little improvements you made. Like a true Stoic, you need to sit down and place your case in your court. Self-examination and reviewing your day will make you a better person day-by-day. Judge your actions and try to ensure not to repeat your mistakes. A good person is more than happy to get advice. On the other hand, a weak man always shows resentment towards guidance.

This routine will immensely enhance your mindfulness and attention, which is the prerequisite in practicing Stoicism effectively. If you wish to boost yourself all times, the awareness of what you do is a must. Otherwise, you may fall into the dangerous zone of reactivity. You will lose your path towards being a Stoic, as you do not know, understand your actions.

This is the reason why everyday reflection routines are pivotal in the Stoic way of thinking. When you do not have a clue where you turned out badly, how are you expected to improve personally? You do not know how you need to act on the planet. How can you become your better self?

For instance, one night, you know that you responded like a yank when the other driver crossed your path, and you caused a ruckus. Next time when you end up in a similar circumstance, and in case you are careful enough, you choose to improve and remain quiet, persistent and pardoning. This is an easy decision. Take five minutes each day to intentionally review your day and your activities. What did you progress nicely? What not, really? Did something bother you? Did you experience outrage, begrudge, dread? How might you improve the next time?

Joined with the Stoic morning schedule, this is simply the ideal improvement strategy: Your psychological readiness joined with self-investigation will prompt persistent learning and self-development. In addition, it will make you more aware of your activities. Continuously remain kind and forgiving. Give some self-empathy. You are making an honest effort. That is everything you need to do. What is more, regardless of whether you do not feel well, that is ordinary. Everyone battles and encounters mishaps. Acknowledge this: consistently be thinking to yourself.

1.6 Night Routine

Your night routine might include journaling to reflect upon your day, contemplation, and then finally going to sleep.

Journaling

Journaling has always remained a crucial part of all philosophical streams like Stoicism too. Journaling before going to bed has numerous benefits. It empties and frees your mind. It gives you ample time to stop and breathe. Putting your thoughts, hopes, and fears onto paper clear the mind and heart and give way to new ideas. Your journal routine at night will track your daily professional and personal endeavors. Whatever you are chasing, the routine of journaling will help in making it more clear and celebrating the small wins, assessing bumps, and staying focused all along.

Epictetus teachings advise you to ask questions to yourself before going to bed to review your actions. He asks you to mark the duties which are yet to be done to ensure you complete them as soon as you wake up. The self-analysis in the night will also help you in gaining control over the negative emotions as you subconsciously aware of the fact that you will be judged and questioned by night. In this way, you learn to lessen anger and other negative emotions.

Look Thoughtfully

Whether the day was easy or tough, or a success or failure, there will always be a chance to have perspective in the end. Look at the sky and the stars, the moon, and the clouds. Imagine yourself up there and floating high above the earth. Then, look down; see how tiny it looks from there. Look thoughtfully at the vastness and the millions of years passed on this planet before this moment. The struggles of your daily life will look small when you change your context.

Sleep

Remind yourself that you did really well today. You gave your best. Let the fate handle from here. You should be focused on what is within your reach and control. Make the most out of your day and time available to you. Then, put the head down. Go to sleep with peace. Get sleep until you are well-rested, then get ready and welcome the next day.

The practical stoic practices given in this chapter are not hard to implement during a day. You can easily follow these practices to make yourself more in control of who you are. After developing these simple routines, you will start to notice how content they will make you. These routines will surely have a huge impact on your life.

Chapter 2: The Best Stoicism Exercises

Stoicism is not a theoretical philosophy. It is about having a practical approach towards life and its events. The most crucial part is to learn how to do it. Merely learning the theoretical aspect of the Stoic philosophy is not enough to become a genuine Stoic. Ancient Stoic philosophers did not just give teachings. They also practiced what they preached.

Adopting Stoicism in life might be a little bit challenging in the beginning. Therefore, you must be persistent throughout the journey. Today we all live in a world where many people have been looking out to link themselves to some ideology. They hope the ideology of Stoicism will help them in making sense of all the chaos that exists in this world. But it will only work in lessening your suffering if you practice the stoic exercises given below to free yourself.

2.1 The Obstacle is the Way

You can only control your own actions and thoughts. You cannot control other things and circumstances. This is why the Stoics adopted a reserve clause in their actions. The main idea behind it is that you do whatever you have to do to get that goal. But keep this fact in mind that some things would not be in your control. Therefore, you need to have the reserve clause too, like "God willing."

In other words, if you want to achieve something, keep reminding yourself that there would be some obstacles. It will give you help in making peace with the outcome because you admit that it is not in your control. You should not confuse your aspirations with the functionality of the universe. There will be obstacles. It does not mean sitting back and not trying. These obstacles will tell you how far you can go. They will reveal who you are. One particular obstacle can give you a new way and a different perspective to see the world.

It requires that one should give the best to whatever one does. Embrace what is in control, and let it go of what is not. You should know that the outcome is beyond anyone's control. So, whenever you plan to do something, just make use of a reserve clause. Train yourself to see and accept the obstacles and find something from whatever is on your plate.

You can see whatever you are reluctant to accept completely as just an obstacle, and when you face an obstacle, either stand there still and stare to curse your fate, or accept that obstacle and handle it to deal expeditiously. The Stoic philosopher and the Roman emperor Marcus Aurelius always recommended the later approach. He suggested that you should handle any obstacle you find in your way quickly. Do not waste time in complaining about it.

2.2 Practicing Poverty

This teaching tells you to live as simply as you can. So how can you live simply in this modern age? Choosing a simple lifestyle does not mean one has to abandon certain things. It is a rather negative approach to think like that as it will leave you feeling unfulfilled and empty. Stoicism has advocated a positive view. It is your state of mind that determines the perspective on possessions and wealth. Your wealth is nothing else, just the habit of your mind. When you choose to train your minds to look at what you have is more than enough, you escape the vicious cycle of wants to become more content. You become a wise person when you stop grieving for something which you do not have. Instead, appreciate the things that you have.

The most crucial thing is to practice poverty. Choose certain days when you love to have the cheapest fare, rough dress, and everything you fear. It will make you immune as your soul would toughen itself. You would be ready beforehand for stressful occasions. It is about living the worst-case scenarios. Leave the things that feed your ego. Repeat it again and again. Start from less, then increase the number of days.

Make it an important part of your life, as it is not that hard to apply. For example, you can do three consecutive days of fasting to expose yourself to the unfamiliar and real hunger sensation. You can schedule your time of fasting periods as per your convenience in the beginning. In the end, you will be in a mental state that will make you feel even more content. It would prove to be an experience that will free you from your worst fears.

Practicing poverty or living your fears and worst-case scenarios in your real life are fruitful in the long term. It is not about just journaling or thinking about things in the head. It is about real exposure to suffering and pain to develop your tolerance and endurance. The more we practice poverty and discomfort by our own choice, the less unplanned and unexpected discomfort will control and affect your life.

Mastering your appetite for drink and food is just the beginning. It is the base of self-control. Building temperance is among the cardinal virtues. You have many easy events to do it daily, like every time you sit and eat. That is what you should mindfully try at mealtime. It can prove to be not just beneficial for the soul but also for your physical health.

2.3 Retreat and Reconnect

People always search for retreats and renewals for themselves, by the coast or in a hill station. It might work, but what they do not understand is that it is nowhere but in mind, a person itself. That is the place where you can find a trouble-free and peaceful retreat. So, give yourself a retreat and continuously renew yourself. It perfectly describes the current scenario.

The first retreat that people find in this age is the digital one. That is how we find an escape by retreating ourselves into social media and technology. But the best way to thrive and finding peace is taking a break from the busy world and making time to renew yourself by creating reconnection to yourself.

2.4 Negative Visualization

Keep asking yourself about what could go more wrong. What can happen to be the worst? That is a classic example of living a life according to Stoicism. It is at the heart of being a Stoic. Preparing for any worst-case scenario that could happen and always handling it with smartness and calm should be your goal. Many people love to do the planning, and when that does not go as they have imagined it to be, they go through an emotional breakdown. It is not recommended as it will not help you. So, it should be prevented.

Just always be prepared for the bad stuff. Visualize that so that as it happens in the future, you will be better able to handle and accept it. It is not that you will suffer less loss by doing this, but you would not freak out. Nobody wants the worst-case scenario to happen and exist in the real life, but one should be prepared for it. If you already have imagined the inconvenient situation, you will stay calmer and composed and thus get the best out of it.

You get devastated when you do not expect something to happen. Ask yourself about the planning you have in the coming days. Do negative visualization about what can go wrong. In this way, you will have a much smarter response. The Stoics try to focus more on things that are under their control. Fate is not one of those things. So, it is advisable not to look for a different reality. Instead, accept things as they are.

The wise person is like a dog who runs joyfully with a moving cart and smoothly keeps pace. On the other hand, a foolish person is like the dog who grumbly struggles with the leash and is dragged with the cart. We cannot change that happens to all of us in our lives. So, why not try the smartest thing and accept it. There is no point in showing resentment and fighting everything that comes our way. We are exactly like a dog who is leashed to the cart. Therefore, we should enjoy our journey than being dragged along. When we show resentment, we wrongly assume that we had a choice.

Practice asking yourself when things happen to you, whether you could have done something or not. Answer honestly. If not, accept fate's control. There is no sense at all to go and fight with reality. It will make you just feel miserable. Practice being nonjudgmental. Do not judge events and people. Just accept all of it as how they are. Do not attach to things. Things will always go, so do not get so much attached.

2.5 Practice Accepting What Life Gives You

Embracing reality is what acceptance teaches us. It is the conscious decision to experience life as it is instead of trying to change things as you want. Practice acceptance as whatever you are not accepting will only cause you pain. Your non-acceptance will make it even worse. You might be facing a really painful experience in life, but running from acceptance will surely lead you into an abyss.

Desiring this world, its people and circumstances work according to your wishes and be something that is not what it is frustrating, draining, and demoralizing. Acceptance will allow you to move on from a perpetually stuck position. Among the fundamental maxims, ad beliefs of Stoicism philosophy are the main idea of not focusing on things that are not under your control. This is what the most amazing practitioners of the philosophy of Stoicism put it.

One way of being content in life is to stop worrying about the things that are out of our will-power. Ruminating and complaining about those things is useless and irrational. Rather, when you focus on circumstances within your control, your attitude, habits, interpretation, and actions, it will make a lot of positive difference.

You should challenge yourself about the things under your control. For instance, let's say you have suffered a huge disappointment recently, and you have realized that there is nothing more you can do about it. Then what should you do? Start by making a list. Include all things that you can possibly think of, which are under your control—then think about the challenges you can give to yourself that fall within the list. For instance, you are overweight by some pounds, so you challenge yourself that you will shed those extra pounds. Then look at the things under your control. Starting a regime of exercise and changing your eating patterns are the two things under your control.

You cannot always fix the situation or event that disappoints you. What you can do is to fix the issue of being overweight, so simply focus on what you can and accept what you cannot. It is all about prioritizing things and shifting your attention.

2.6 Do not Try to Control Your Surroundings

One of the pivotal pieces of advice to Stoicism teaching is to recognize the fact that you need to let go of the desire to control your surroundings. You can control your emotions, responses, and thoughts. But do not be dragged down by this misconception that you have control over outside events and circumstances. According to Marcus Aurelius, you will find your real strength when you understand your mind and let go of the desire to control outside events.

When we are unable to control our surroundings, there is an anger, expectation, sadness, anxiety, jealousy, fear, and envy. Through experiencing these emotions, we tend to respond out of character that can lead to some regretful choices. So, learn to remain calm by controlling emotions, and also watch how the decisions you make, stand on the firm ground in the long term. If you desire to escape things that bother you, you need to become a different person, not be in a different place.

2.7 Stop Complaining About Your Life

According to Marcus Aurelius teaching, do not let your mind possess things that are not yours. Rather, count your blessings that you possess. You will realize this if you think about what you would do if you do not have them. Watch yourself in valuing those things before you lose them. All ancient Stoics used to be minimalists. They always chose to value things they had rather than longing for things they did not have. They always showed gratefulness in life. They focused on whatever they had rather than unnecessarily desiring for other things.

This is exactly what you should do. You should try to fight your urge to gather and hold unnecessary stuff. Be grateful for whatever you already have without being getting attached to things. They can go away at any time. Ask yourself how much you want things you already have in case you do not have them. Just like other exercises given in this book, write down your list. For instance, write down 3-4 things you are genuinely grateful for. Just do not buy things you do not need. Then appreciate things and blessings you possess.

2.8 Write Your Thoughts

Try not to go to sleep until you have reviewed your deeds. Ask yourself what have you erred, or what is it that is complete or yet to be done. Start writing and review your actions. Do this exercise honestly, and you will realize how much clarity you will get out of it. You can write your thoughts in the morning, evening, or even before sleep at night, or simply choose any quiet moment. Write whenever you feel like writing or whenever your desire to write arises.

The point here is just to look upon your actions of the day. It is morally and ethically salient, appreciate your right deeds, learn from mistakes, and make notes if you want to and move far away from things that can disturb your peace of mind.

2.9 Practice Forgiveness

The philosophy of Stoicism believes that we all try to do things as we think them to be right. Even it might not be right. People do not do something wrong deliberately and on purpose. We all just act what we think something as right. We should show empathy rather than playing the blame game. We do not need to be angry with someone who can not differentiate between right or wrong. We all should be kinder and more tolerant.

Forgive yourself and others too. Do not remember the wrongs of others. Before getting angry, try to step back and see that the other person did not know better. But if you do, then you should be forgiving and kind. Do not seek any revenge when someone wrongs you. Choose to stay kind and be tolerant. Show empathy rather than demeaning the wrongdoers. They are just blinded in mind. If you suffer meanness from others, try to take it as your training. We all have been trying to learn and get better. Rough patches will happen. So, leave them behind and then move on. It is just part of your training.

2.10 Never Stop Learning and Practicing

Philosophers always warn people not to be ever satisfied with learning. You should always add practice to whatever you think. Train yourself as hard as you can. As time passes, most people forget what they learned and then end up on the opposite side. Their opinions go in the opposite direction of where they should have been. Stoicism demand practicing from you. Practice everything that you have known and learned. Do not become satisfied with just skimming over your exercises. You should choose one exercise at a time and start immediately.

If you do not learn things to put them immediately in practice, then you do not learn anything. So, get started immediately. Choose any of the exercises given in this book and start practicing without wasting any time in arguing about the qualities of a good person. Be the one.

2.11 View from above

As Marcus Aurelius said in Meditations that all the agitations that trouble you are just superfluous. They all depend upon your own judgments. You can easily leave them permanently by mere embracement of the universe and comprehending its eternity and then imagining the undeniable swiftness of all changes. In this way, you will realize how brief the real passage from your birth to death was.

Marcus's teachings have always invited people to take distance once in a while from their daily life, preoccupations, and stresses. Purposeful embracement of a view from above will make you put and see life from a different perspective. The break can be in terms of space or time. You will realize that the apparently serious problems are nothing but just a blip. You can also practice this exercise by just visualizing or writing about it.

When you are beset by something, just try to do this exercise. You will notice that it is our imagination that gets into unnecessary troubles. You might mess up and totally forget that there is not anything big enough compared to life itself. You might focus on things and think that it is important, but the fact is that nothing can be as crucial as it looks when we think about it. That is when perspective can prove to be a life-saver and helpful. Just try to look at the view from some distance. Imagine you are at some high place, then try to look at yourself just as a dot living in just a small house, city, and country. Then compare it to the perspective of the whole universe.

Our whole planet itself is so tiny relative to our universe. Our problems are not really as big as we think in this grand view of life. From a distance, things will seem trivial, which will help you in seeing them from an indifferent perspective. You will notice that everything in this world is just fleeting. Try to look at problems that every single person is concerned about; if someone has a fever and is concerned about this while in some other part of the world people are just hit by the Tsunami, or people getting into the bomb explosions.

The headache will look like a real joke from a distance. This holds true for all other problems as well. Just Imagine for a second that you are rising higher in the sky. From there, you look down on things and yourself. Go as higher as you can, then look at our planet. Just remind yourself you live down there.

2.12 Memento Mori

Prepare your mind as if you have reached the end of your life. Postpone nothing. Learn to balance the books of your life each day. When you do that and put the finishing touches to your life every day, you will never face the time limitation problem. This is something that everyone desperately needs and should implement in their own lives. It is one such idea and thought that people would rather ignore. They will avoid it and then pretend like it is untrue. It is a fact that our ego stays away from things that reflect reality. As we have created our own reality, so everything that goes against the comfort zone we have built for ourselves will not attract us. We are just petrified and do not want to see life's reality as it is. That is the reason we are scared to do meditation and reflect on things.

Death is inevitable. Such reminders are related to Memento Mori, which is an ancient practice. It reflects on mortality. This philosophy is linked to Socrates, who used to say that the real practice of philosophical thinking is nothing but the acceptance of the reality of death. In Buddhist texts, one term that is very prominent is maraṇasati – which means 'remember death.' Many ancient Sufis were named "people of graves," as they mostly focused on one's mortality and death.

This thinking will make you depressed if you keep missing the point and real idea behind it. It is an effective tool to create meaning and priority. It is one such tool that many generations used in creating urgency and real perspective. Learn to treat your limited time as a gift and do not waste on some trivial issues. Death does not make our life pointless. Rather, it makes it purposeful.

Fortunately, you do not need to die to grasp this fact. One simple reminder is enough to bring you closer to live your desired life. It does not matter what your reality is or how much you left undone. A car might hit you anyway. It is what it is. It could be all over. Today or someday soon.

2.13 Cultivate Philanthropy

Philanthropy is all about a strong desire to work for people's welfare. Modern thinking suggests you can become a philanthropist through your money. But this is not true. Anyone can be a philanthropist. The thinking behind it requires the right attitude. We human beings like to live in an enclosed series of some kind of spheres. Each sphere shows a greater distance from who we are as a person.

To cultivate philanthropy in your life, your goal must be trying and bringing everyone into a closed circle. As you consider your family just your extension, similarly, think of fellow citizens also your family. Expand your mind and heart and think of the whole of humanity as your part. One Stoic philosopher even emphasized considering our siblings to be parts of our body, just like a leg or an arm.

It requires a huge shift in your perspective. Put effort into it. It has a lot of advantages. You will not become unnecessarily attached to one individual that will cause you less pain on their death or departure from life. A large circle of close friends means high exposure to different viewpoints and cultures. It is an amazing opportunity to learn and connect. Just randomly approach a stranger, and start a healthy and pleasant conversation. Let people and your friends know that you consider all of them as part of the family. They should come back to you as such.

2.14 Practice Detachment

Marcus Aurelius wrote about amor fati, which is in the Latin language. It means 'love of fate.' Nietzsche, a revolutionary philosopher, expressed that his formula for the greatness of a person is this concept; Amor fati. He said no one wants anything to be forward, backward, or any different. When you worry, you do because of the desired outcome. You get really anxious thinking about the unfolding of the future in a way you have not imagined. But the truth is that you cannot control the outcome.

Amor fati teaches you to do the most you can to put all your best efforts, making this world a much better place, and doing so without being worried about the results. When you embrace this Stoicism philosophy called Amor fati, you embrace your future, your fate, and whatever it might turn out. It does not say to become pessimistic or nihilistic — expecting the worst or doing nothing for a belief that everything is going to be worthless.

Adopt Amor fati and simply love your fate without giving up your goals. Work towards what is needed and intended to be done. Do it without unnecessarily linking yourself to any results or outcomes. It is about accepting the results, whatever it might be, because you can control its process, not the outcome. The philosophy of Stoicism believes that the entire universe is rationally and perfectly organized, including all events happening in time. It is all preordained and meant to happen. So, fighting against the cosmic fate will cause unhappiness.

The best option is embracing the outcome with love. Work and try to get the best of it. Consider it as the arrow you have aimed at, with balance and best technique, but not to be worried about its ending point. Accept it with serenity, and then keep moving with the intention of getting better with every next shot. Do not demand things and events to happen according to your wish. Rather, embrace how they happen and remain content.

Chapter 3: Mastering Self-Control

We live in times with constant fear, uncertainty, and doubt. We need a strong perspective and self-control to go through these hard times. We need to see what a situation can teach us. Tough times always make us feel like the whole world is crushing on us. Life will never stop evolving and moving. Time heals everything. We will always find ourselves prepared to face life again. But we all have to find our own way. Sufferings and hardships are just part of life. A crisis happens to make us grow as a person and makes us better, but it happens only when we go ahead with the right mindset.

Self-control and discipline are the fundamental mindset, action, and philosophy that keep a person in a specific routine. Self-control helps a person in achieving whatever he/she wants to pursue. Stoicism is not about reading or talking dense books. It is more than that which helped humans throughout history in reaching their professional and personal achievements. The wisdom behind it is still intact. That is why it is considered as the most popular and practical philosophy. In this chapter, we will differentiate between the things that are under our control and the things that are not under our control. So that you can get a better idea of where to put your focus on.

3.1 Self-control Practicing

When you have self-control, you become stronger. You do not get stuck in the past. You have clarity in your communication. You start to forgive as you know that is the only way to grow in life. See your life as a blessing. Never forget to enjoy it. You need to learn and accept that you have no control over external circumstances, but you do have enough control over how you react to those circumstances. Life is short and fragile. So, spend time here wisely by appreciating life more. Science shows that choosing challenges stimulates the growth of cells in our brain, which helps in coping and building resilience.

Marcus Aurelius is considered a powerful man in the world. Being in that position, if he had chosen to do something, nothing would have gone off-limits. Marcus Aurelius was a devoted student of Stoicism's philosophy who practiced Stoicism all his life. During his ruling period, he constructed autobiographical writings, known as "Meditations", in which he offered many key insights on building self-control and self-discipline.

Marcus Aurelius believed in hard work as this is what we are supposed to do as human beings, then there is nothing left to complain about. He believed that there is a purpose in our existence. We have all been created for something. It is up to us to find out our purpose because we need it to wake up and go to work each morning. In other words, Marcus Aurelius advised to do the tasks without whining.

Be responsible for your life. The mentality of 'why always me' needs to be changed as it is hindering you from getting mental toughness. It might not be our fault, but the life depends entirely on determining the things within our control and take responsibility for those things, and determining things that are not under our control and let them go. We have to train ourselves to frame the things we can control instead of resorting to a useless self-pity mentality.

Self-control will free you from pawning off blame on other people when things go wrong. You can only do this for those with having mental fortitude. Be the person who can step in and practice self-control while taking action. Do not become that person who looks at things with the intention of blaming someone. When we victimize ourselves or our current situation, we relinquish control. We deliberately absolve ourselves of any personal responsibility. Self-control and ownership of our life events give meaning to our lives. Let's identify the things we have control over and the things that are out of our control.

Things You Cannot Change or Control in Your Life

Most people are not content in their lives because of the non-acceptance of the circumstances or things that they are unable to change or control. It leads to frustration, suffering, and disappointment. You should have enough serenity in your life where you can accept what you cannot change in your life and courage to control or the things you can. What is more important is to have the wisdom to differentiate them. It is a simple philosophy. Stoicism teaches you to put your focus, energy, and time on those parts of your life that you can change, but at the same time, accept those you cannot.

Unfortunately, most people do not make any effort to make that change happen in those aspects that make them unhappy. Instead, they put their efforts into changing those that cannot be controlled. It is not that hard to change things that are the cause of dissatisfaction through actions. For instance, if you have extra pounds, you can easily change that as it is under your control. If you hate your job, just change it. If you are not content in any relationship, just take a stand, and change it. If you want more friends, you can make new ones. The choice has always been yours.

It is crucial to know about things you cannot change in your life, no matter what. Wisdom is to know what you cannot change and what you can. You should focus on your efforts in changing or controlling what you can and to accept what you cannot. By doing this, you will find peace, happiness, freedom, and serenity. Let's discuss those things:

Opinions of Other People

Most people believe that they can change the thinking, perceptions, and opinions of other people. But this is not true. It will never happen. Your efforts to do that will go in vain while trying to change the thoughts and opinions of others. People can have opinions and say what they choose to think. You have absolutely no control in that aspect. You can just control your thinking, perceptions, and opinions. Getting upset over the words and opinions of others is pointless. People will have their opinions, and you cannot change it.

Actions of Other People

You have no control over what people do. They have their independent personality, and they act according to that. Your actions are based on who you are. Despite this, many people spend their time and efforts to get friends, family members, and spouses to act as they want them to act.

Feelings of Other People

You can affect people's feelings, as feelings are a consequence of thoughts just like you cannot control how people think, you cannot control how people feel. So, you cannot change other people's feelings. For instance, when you give a gift to someone, how the other person receives and perceives it is not under your control. It is great to be sensitive and show empathy towards how people are feeling, but drop the idea of controlling or changing it.

Your Age

Aging reminds us of how precious time is. Each day as we grow older, get us closer to our death, which is inevitable. You cannot control this, even though most people fight and deny this phenomenon.

Your Past

It is where most people get stuck. There is no way to go back to the past and fix things. You cannot undo what is done. We all make mistakes, so the wisest approach should be to learn and move on. You cannot undo your past. Getting stuck in the past will lead to a life full of regrets. You have the present moment. Accept your past to free yourself. Just like your past, you do not have any control over your origin, where you came from, your background, etc. do not have much importance to it as where you come from should not limit what you can achieve in life.

We all suffer in the hands of someone or by something throughout our lives. These wounds and pain often hurt even after they have all passed. But you cannot change it. The idea of keeping that in our hearts and getting revenge will never heal your wounds. Keep reminding yourself that it is not possible to reverse time and undo any situation. Retribution and hate will only weigh you down. It only impedes on your happiness. Train yourself to accept the transition, learn from it, and then move on. Lost time and opportunities are gone forever. There is no way to regain them. So, make yourself a promise today, stop wasting time, and start training yourself to let go of your past.

Our Family

Nobody chooses one's, family members. You did not have any choice in where you be born. Your mother, father, siblings, and extended family just become part of your life from your birth. You will always be linked with them. If you want happiness, you should accept who your family is. It does not imply that you must tolerate an abusive person. It just means you cannot change what it is in this regard.

The happiness of other People around You

Pleasing everyone is not possible. While you may please people for a time, but it will not last for too long. Most people tend to waste their lives to please all people around them. When you do this, you do at the expense of your own happiness and peace of mind. The sooner you stop trying this useless effort to please people, the sooner you will be liberated. First, focus on your own happiness.

Today's world has become overly materialistic. Most people keep focusing on their neighbors, society, and friends at large. They wish to go ahead of everyone. It will only lead them to want a new car, a bigger house, and more luxuries. In the back of their head is to please and impress people with these things. Accept the fact that there will be some differences. We are all unique, so you should love who you are instead of trying to please everyone.

Making People Love You

Sometimes you will not get love in return. Remind yourself that this is not under your control, as real love holds no conditions in return. Genuine love should be unconditional. So, stop trying to accomplish this impossible desire to change someone's opinion and make that person love you. You can do everything for someone to please his/her in all ways, but still, you cannot force love on someone. Instead, some people do not understand this basic fact and spend their energy and time to earn someone's love.

Your Appearance

You can wear a stylish dress and exercise for losing weight or getting bigger muscles. That is in your hands. But you cannot control or change the way you look. Your height, body type, looks, and skin color are the features you should accept, embrace, and love. Make a healthy relationship with the way you look. The more you accept yourself, the happier you will be. This confidence and self-acceptance will make you even more attractive.

Pain

We all feel pain and suffering at one point or the other in life. It might be emotional, psychological, or physical pain. We all fall down. We face disease and disappointments. It is just all part of our lives. Accept that the pain cannot be avoided, but sufferings associated with that pain are optional and in our hands. When you accept this fact that we all experience pain, then you do not hold any expectation to become pain-free. Spending countless hours thinking about that pain will only make it worse.

Things You Can Change or Control in Your Life

You might not change a lot of things in your life. But there are other things that are under your control. That process starts with accepting what you cannot change and then work on things under your control. Let's look at those things that you can change and lead a content life.

Accept Your Past Choices, Change Your Future Ones

Making mistakes in life is inevitable. These are learning opportunities. As you walk through your life, sometimes you might have to learn the hard way. But not punish yourself about it. Just learn from your past. Then use it as a guide for the future. When we know better about things, we do them better.

Change Your Negative Surrounding

You cannot trust everyone in life, and it is the bitter truth of all. Some people do not want to cause your pain or hurt you, but some do. You just need to forgive them. It is a gift that you give to yourself. Let go of negative energies. It does not serve you anything. Make fresh choices about whom you should spend your time with. Kick those negative energy vampires out of life. People who drain all of your energy should not be part of your life. Only positive, growth-oriented, and uplifting people should be in your lives.

It might be difficult sometimes to accept your family members when they make life unpleasant. They may be critical, demanding, or judgmental. You cannot change them. What you can do is to change your view about them. However, if some friends are showing negative behavior, make a choice, and walk away. Find better and positive companions.

Change Your Unhealthy Lifestyle

All you should do is to accept your appearance. Love yourself the way you are. What you can change is your unhealthy lifestyle. Change your exercise and eating patterns.

You will start to feel much better. Do not go into the trap of "imperfections" or this society's beauty standards. First, look at the inner beauty and shine from within by having a healthy lifestyle.

Change Your Life's Journey

The blessings shine in the dark moments. Be like those someone who turned his/her painful sufferings into a meaningful path – not just for themselves but for others too. You might have dealt darkest moments in your life, but the journey never ends there. Have goals in your life and improve them to grow. Positive change always starts with accepting how things are. When you show resistance, you put negative energy into your situation and this world.

It is more productive and effective to put energy into change than resistance, which is pointless as it will keep you stuck. Move towards the positive change. Keep in mind that life can be a tricky balance between change and acceptance. With action and conscious focus, you can accept and then change for good.

3.2 Practice Controlling Your Desires

Ending your desires will your mind just revolving around itself. You need to find a goal so that you could build a practical plan to take action. If you have a desire for something that is not in your control, you will face disappointment. Even things you can control and under favorable circumstances, should not be deserving of your desire. Restrict yourself and exercise your powers within detachment and discipline.

Late Stoics believed in mainly three areas where you can train yourself. The first is related to detachment and desires. The second is related to impulsion to act or not. It is mainly associated with the duty that you may act for good reasons. The third one is related to freedom from composure, deception, and judgment. The most urgent one is the one that is associated with passions as strong emotions only arise when you fail in your aversions and desires.

How can you just sit around, hoping, waiting, begging, and craving for a change in the situation to happen? You hope that you will find the right person, and at the same time, you remain unsocial and maintain your old habits. You wish, you could lose some weight without working for it. You want your talent to be well-recognized, but you hold yourself back from trying.

Marcus Aurelius believed that action and principles should be the only source of your desire. It should be restricted to what is in your control. Nature thrives on forward progress, and for a logical mind, it means not to accept uncertainty or falsehood in perceptions. Make unselfish actions the only aim, and shun the things you have control over. In other words, what you require in your forward progress journey is a deliberate action. There is no hope for any uncertainties. Deliberate action requires your consideration and deliberation, not your desire.

Leave the desire for amateurs. Live your life on actions, not on hoping for things to happen as you wish. Attach yourself to process, not outcome. Prepare well and then act. Then, you can do amazing things. Have clarity in your mind, goal, and actions, and do not become a slave of your desires.

3.3 Practice Controlling Your Opinion

Just take a break and ask yourself, what have your thoughts and opinions done to you? Was having so many opinions and perspectives about everything around you worthy enough? The digital media has made all of us believe that we all need to have views on everything. Is it necessary to be full of useless opinions? Loneliness might be one of the reasons in this new world. We all feel lonely at some point despite having people around us.

It all has built the urge to be right all the time. It does not matter how you make others feel by doing so. But have you ever thought that do your opinions and views make you feel empowered? Or are they just a burden on you? When someone forms an opinion about something and then thinks about sharing it, he/she starts to think of the imaginary arguments that he would use to prove his point to others. You keep a check on those arguments just to see who responded and who did not. The result will be your anger, or you might feel offended. All this leads you away from your goal.

As mentioned earlier, there are things you cannot change. If you keep fighting and show resistance, then you will cause your own suffering. It is not that particular situation that causes suffering. It is you who is resisting it, which will cause pain. So, you are left with two choices: keep fighting what you do not like and ultimately suffer, or accept what it is and change your opinion about it.

Your shallow thoughts will cause inner turmoil inside of you. The bubble is meant to burst if you rely on superficial knowledge. But you are not ready to accept the facts as opposed to your opinions. You might emerge victorious from all this. But your inner self will feel like easting itself. The reason is that your mind is still tugging and imploring to make you consider other perspectives. This turmoil will turn into stress.

To eliminate your pain that comes with unnecessary opinions, fix its cause. Eliminate all pointless opinions by asking yourself that it is useful. Or is it worth your time? If a lot of things interests you, is it necessary to go in-depth about all of them? The more we put our focus on useless things and opinions, the less focus we give to ourselves to go deeper for the useful things.

Gradually, you will find peace within a deeper focus on useful things. The world does just fine even without your opinions. Accept this fact, and it will make you feel invisible and liberated. Distance yourself from all unimportant events. It will definitely help you live a healthier life. You would not lose your valuable energy on events that do not impact you. You will rather channelize your energy more constructively. Do not try to silence your heart. Listen to your heart and practice controlling your opinions. Give it a try and see the results.

3.4 Practice Controlling Aversion

Many people do not realize that they have a great tendency to dislike things. They spent most of their life avoiding things they do not like. We do not realize it, but we all have this tendency of aversion. It is not an issue to have them, but if you drive by those aversions, you lock yourself into a very limited life. For instance, if you do not like vegetables, it is hard to have a healthy diet. Similarly, if you do not like exercise, it is difficult to be healthy and strong.

Aversions are not always bad. Some of them can prove to be useful, like hating being abused or having unhealthy food. But they also have the tendency to restrict you in many ways. That can make you unhappy if your life is not free of things you are averse to. So do not let your aversions control you and your happiness.

To do that, you need to know your aversions. Make a list of those things that you hate, avoid, and cannot stand them—for instance, foods, behaviors, websites, frustrating situations, or social situations. There are many examples like that, so start making a list. When you list down your aversion, then notice them and face them. Notice how they feel to your body. What is its energy or sensation? Open yourself to that feeling. Do not run away from that. Do not reject it immediately. Embrace it, and remain curious. Many people ignore them, but you are the one who is willing to go deeper.

You are free to add vegetables to your diet or have a conversation with annoying people. You can do this all without being falling apart. If you remain focused during the situations, you will learn to appreciate their beauty. You will be able to embrace those aversions rather than ignoring them. It is all part of the human experience, and there is nothing to be panicked about. You can free yourself from being in a fixed mind. Be flexible. You can go through your aversions and desires with joy, love, and appreciation for all blessings.

3.5 Practice Controlling Your Words

Words have immense power. So, learn to control your words so that they can be used just for good. Here you will be given [practical advice on how you can do that. Keep in mind that there is no need to express every thought. We have been living in such a world that pushes us to use our voice. It makes you believe that you have every right heard. But too many opinions and words will cause you no benefit. You need to be sensible in using your words. It is quite easy to get trapped in debates.

If you have an interest in something, and you think if you could explain things more, the other person is more likely to get it. It is a wrong perspective to even think like that. Silence has power. There is no need to use a lot of words or raise your voice to make your point valid. Well-structured words have great power, and power should be handled carefully. Kind words have the ability to soothe the soul. While on the other hand, harsh words feel like a sharp knife.

The gentle words are like a tree that supports life, while deceitful words crush someone's spirit. Many people love to make some cutting remarks. On the other hand, wise words have healing power. One gentle answer can deflect the anger. One harsh word can cause tempers flare. Your tongue and your words bring life or death. Whatever you talk about, you will see its consequences.

Speak but not for the sake of the world. You do not have to function as per this world's demand. You will find many places where you should control your words and tongue. Just ask yourself honestly, whether it is worth or not. Controlling your words is something you can fully master if you have clarity in your mind. Promise yourself that you will speak only where you have to speak.

3.6 Practice Controlling Your Actions

According to Marcus Aurelius, one must build one's life by actions and then be content with the result, whatever it is. Some people have not just a solid purpose and also a practical plan; still, almost 95% fail in achieving their goals. One might fail because of a lack of fail consistency. You have to get up every day to put effort into your work. The act of consistently showing up to work on your craft will do wonders in terms of building endurance. You will build focus and achieve something great.

One has to put countless hours before reaping benefits. Self-Discipline and self-control are just the habit of being consistent and finding your motivation to work on something consistently until you see results. If you do not succeed, it should not define who you are. It does not affect your character. It is one's ability to keep working that to make someone into a strong and disciplined person. If there is one bad day, it does not mean there would be a whole bad week or year. The moment we get up, always remember that a new day in your life is your new life. Move forward and focus on things ahead of you. This is life.

Chapter 4: Be a Stoic in the Workplace

Conflict and collaboration are not opposed to each other. They can go along really well. So, let us banish this notion of high-performing groups being happy people who get along with each other. The healthy rivalry fuels success. How would you keep the workplace strife beneficial? Think carefully when something starts to turn troublesome and step in to keep things from decaying into a poisonous work environment.

When a colleague needs help, what would you do to assist him? Furthermore, how would you establish a workplace where strife and conflict drive progress and accomplishment? Go to the immortal shrewdness of probably the best chief, Marcus Aurelius. In this chapter, you will learn how you can be a stoic at your workplace.

4.1 How Stoic Practices Affect Your Work

Maybe the best ruler, Marcus Aurelius, is broadly viewed as the ideal chief's encapsulation. He composed Meditations. Presently viewed as probably the best work of theory ever, it is an assortment of Aurelius' own musings and ruminations on the Stoic way of thinking. Apathy centers on tolerating what is not inside your control and acing your feelings. Stoics react to struggle with reason and rationale as opposed to enthusiastic upheavals. Winning a contention is futile. Righteousness and character are the only essential things.

The methodology is not tied in with letting people state anything they desire to or about you because, in the end, it does not generally make a difference. It is tied in with perceiving what is genuinely significant and what is not, so you do not let transitory issues occupy you and stop you from accomplishing your best work and being your best self. Among different personalities and egos, "how we get things done around here" — that is the thing that Stoics look to disregard.

Disagreements are an unavoidable aspect of the working environment. Aurelius' Meditations offer sage astuteness for the present chiefs searching for methodologies to utilize that contention to drive achievement. Here are some ways to look at conflicts and disagreements in the workplace from a Stoic's perspective.

Clashes are Inevitable

The struggle does not generally happen because people are troublesome, yet in some cases, it does. Consciences, terrible perspectives, and workplace issues are a reality of corporate life. Like it or not, some people will make your life troublesome just because they are only worried about making theirs more straightforward. Start your day with the fact that you will experience some pushback, and it would not irritate you as much when it occurs. Envision that others will scrutinize your choices, burn through your time, and exploit your readiness to help.

By anticipating this conduct, you can intellectually plan, figure out how to abstain from getting sucked into time-squandering assignments and conversations, and have the option to legitimize your choices when addressed. If things go in a way that is better than anticipated, you will be charmingly amazed.

Life Goes on

One of the central principles of Aurelius' ways of thinking is that nothing remains still. To cite an altogether different sort of logician, "Life moves pretty quickly." This is not intended to be discouraging — indeed, it is meant to be free. Why burn through valuable time and energy getting irritated with things that do not really make a difference? This viewpoint can shield you from getting worked up over issues that will just divert you from things that really matter.

Obsessing Makes It Worse

Outrage just aggravates an awful circumstance. Getting ticked off that somebody patronized you during a gathering does not help — it just disturbs you more. Not only that, it delays the circumstance. What ought to have been a minor blip on your radar abruptly turns into an obsession, as you remember the second again and again. You have already gained zero ground on your work before you know it since you are too bustling stewing.

Opinions do not Matter

Who cares what everybody thinks about you and your work? By the day's end, you are answerable to just a modest bunch of people. Does it make any difference what any other individual thinks about you? Rather than letting it exasperate you, draw certainty from the way that the people whose conclusions genuinely matter — yours and your supervisors — are sure about your work.

Make Criticism Constructive

Try not to make a contention out of criticism. No one is awesome, and no one accomplishes wonderful work. Legitimate self-reflection is an indispensable piece of improvement, and you should invite a wide range of input from a wide range of people. If somebody brings up criticism in your work or thinking, it naturally considers it to be an assault. There is no compelling reason to abide over your inadequacies or feel uncertain about them; accept the open the door to perceive and take care of them.

Take Your Team Members into Confidence

Which would you rather have: a gathering of indifferent "yes" men? Or, on the other hand, a group of people who energetically contend for what they really accept is the best game-plan? Being a decent cooperative person implies provoking others to reveal defective reasoning and cycles. In any case, not every person will concede to what those imperfections are. You should be in struggle with specific groups since you are each upholding for various things.

The account will uphold the most affordable arrangement while promoting will contend for the most responsive. These are both legitimate contemplations: cost viability is similarly as significant as advancement. Others are not contradicting you since they care for you, or because they are a factious individual or incorrect. They are managing their responsibilities.

The best thing for your group is that you address these basic strains head-on. Standardize them. Carry them to the surface to anticipate clashing perspectives and comprehend where they are coming from. Remind the team members that you are all battling for the best results.

Disagreements Can Drive Innovation

In case you are in disagreement with somebody and it really is turning into a detour or keeping you from achieving what you need to accomplish — at that point, discover another way. Use it as an open door for inventive critical thinking, and adjust.

Empowering Productive Conflict

Your group realizes that you are there to listen when they experience something difficult and help them out. It is not something they should mind their own business or stew over peacefully. To begin, it shields your group from clashes or differences. Be straightforward about conversations and discussions occurring at the leader level, particularly about choices that worry them. Just clarify how alternate points of view are calculated into another choice.

In your everyday cooperation, energize disagreeing suppositions and the people who question presumptions. Show your co-workers that differing does not mean they will be viewed as helpless cooperative people or troublesome representatives.

4.2 How to be a Stoic at Your Workplace

A Stoic can discover harmony and lucidity. For a number of years, Stoicism has been a device for the common and rulers as they looked for astuteness, quality, and 'easy street.' It was a theory intended for activity—for practitioners—not for the homeroom. This is why it has been mainstream with everybody; Marcus Aurelius, Seneca, Theodore Roosevelt, Michel de Montaigne, and Frederick. Even football trainers like Pete Carroll and baseball administrators like Jeff Banister have prescribed Stoicism to their players.

How might you receive the rewards of this working framework in your own working environment? It is basic. Go directly to the sources. The following are Stoic activities and methodologies that will help you explore your working environment with better lucidity, adequacy, and significant serenity.

Do not Make Things Unnecessarily Harder

Recollect in life that your obligations are the entirety of individual acts. Focus on each of these as you carry out your responsibility. According to Marcus Aurelius, just deliberately complete your share of work if you are working with a disappointing colleague or a troublesome chief. They request you to do something and because you hate that, you promptly object. There is this issue or that one, or their solicitation is offensive and inconsiderate. So, you let them know, "No, I'm not going to do it." Then they fight back by not doing something that you had recently asked of them. Thus, the contention heightens.

When you could step back and see it equitably, you would likely to observe that not all things requesting are irrational. Some of it is pretty simple to do. Life is sufficiently troublesome. We should not make it harder by getting enthusiastic about inconsequential issues or delving in for fights we do not really think about.

It Might All be in Your Mind

On intense days we may state, "My work is overpowering," or "My supervisor is truly disappointing." Suppose no one, but we could comprehend that this is unthinkable. Somebody cannot disappoint you. Work cannot overpower you. These are outer situations, and they have no admittance to your brain. Those feelings you feel, as genuine as they may be, originate from within, not the outside.

The Stoics utilize the word hypolépsis, which signifies "taking up" — of discernments, musings, and decisions by our psyche. What we expect, what we enthusiastically create in our brain, that is on us. We cannot censure others for causing us to feel focused or disappointed in anything else than we can reprimand them for our envy. The reason is inside us. They are simply the objective.

Have Clarity

We disdain the individual who comes in and attempts to manipulate us around. We tell them that try not to tell us how to dress, how to think, how to manage your responsibility and how to live. This is because we are autonomous, independent people. Or possibly that is the thing that we let ourselves know.

However, when somebody says something we cannot help contradicting. Something inside us reveals to us that we need to contend with them. There is a plate of treats before u. we need to eat them. When somebody accomplishes something we hate, we need to get frantic about it. When something awful occurs, we must be miserable, discouraged, or stressed. In any case, if something great happens a couple of moments later, out of nowhere we are upbeat, energized, and need more.

You could never let someone else jolt you around the manner in which you let your driving forces do. It is time you begin seeing it that way — that you are not manikins that can be made to move along these lines or that way since you feel like it. You ought to be the ones in charge, not your feelings, since you are autonomous, and independent people.

Keep Things Simple

Keep a strong psyche about your job, doing it with exacting and straightforward nobility, love, opportunity, and equity — offering yourself a reprieve from every other thought. You can do this in the event that you approach each undertaking as though it is your last, surrendering each interruption, enthusiastic disruption of reason, and all show, vanity, and grievance over something reasonable. You can perceive how dominance over a couple of things makes it conceivable to carry on with a plentiful and sincere life. Every day presents a new opportunity.

Today, how about you center just on what is before you? Take care of your responsibility. Marcus says to move toward each work as though it were your last, since it could be. Also, regardless of whether it is not, bungling what is directly before you, do not resist anything. Discover lucidity in the straightforwardness of doing things.

It is to Get Consumed by Your Career

How offensive is the attorney whose withering breath passes while at court, at a serious age, arguing for obscure defendants and as yet looking for the endorsement of uninformed observer? At regular intervals, a pitiful display happened in the news. An old tycoon, actually master of his business realm, is prosecuted. Investors and relatives go to court to contend that he is not, at this point intellectually equipped to decide — that the patriarch is not fit to run his own organization and legitimate issues.

Since this amazing individual declined actually to surrender control or build up a progression plan, he is exposed to one of life's most exceedingly terrible embarrassments: the public introduction of his most private weaknesses. It would help if you did not get so enveloped with the work that you believe you are resistant from the truth of maturing and life. Who needs to be the individual who can never give up? Is there so small significance in your life that your solitary interest is to work until you are at the end of hauled away in a casket? Invest wholeheartedly in your work. However, it is not all.

Peace of Mind is Everything

Have empathy, since it encourages you to oversee and thoroughly consider our enthusiastic responses. It can make these sorts of circumstances simpler to endure. It can assist you with overseeing and relieve the triggers that appear to be so continually stumbled. Use Stoicism to deal with the challenges. In any case, remember to ask: Is this actually the existence I need? Each time you get disturbed, a tad of life leaves the body. Are these actually the things on which you need to spend that precious asset? Try not to be hesitant to roll out an improvement — a major one. In the end, it is your peace of mind that matters.

4.3 Dealing with Appearances of Your Co-workers

One of the significant lessons in Stoicism is the way one should comprehend and manage what they term "appearances" or "impression." Generally, these are matters that are outer to the individual to whom they show up. Appearances can undoubtedly deceive us, with the outcome that we feel, figure, consent to, pick or reject, and want or are disinclined to things that we should not to. An empathetic way of thinking gives a few valuable approaches to comprehend and address appearances.

Two pieces of especially valuable guidance relating to this issue are: say to each brutal appearance that you are an appearance and not under any condition what you seem. It is not simply the things that upset people. It is their decisions about those things. We utilize our own ability for self-assurance to oppose naturally taking appearances for real factors, and that similarly, we analyze our decisions to check whether they are precise.

We can force a deferral between enrolling the appearance, and following up on it, or in any event, feeling something towards it. This licenses us a space of time during which we can address the appearance, deciding for ourselves whether it is valid, and how we should manage it. These things are not fortunate or unfortunate in themselves, but rather can have all the remarks of being thus, or can be decided to be so.

Regard People's Differences

Every one of us may move toward life and work in an unexpected way. While it might be a test for a few of us to work with people who dislike the manner in which we do, everybody has the right to have their emotions and qualities regarded.

Think Positive

It is simpler to talk and coexist with people who are positive masterminds and not continually talking contrarily.

Recognize Your Co-workers

Converse with one another on an easygoing premise. You have to have customary discussions with each co-worker; however, recognize their quality and be positive when conversing with them. Here and there, a colleague can be having an awful day, and only one sure remark or praise can make a terrifying day endurable.

Tune in

Tune in to your colleagues when they converse with you. You will never procure regard or comprehend others until you give them your complete consideration.

Acknowledge Others

No individual can or ought to do everything in a work environment. Similarly, as you need backing and thankfulness for the employment you do every day, show a similar thought for your collaborators.

Contribute and Help Out

Try not to let people down when you offer to accomplish a bonus or volunteer for a task. Be cautious, nonetheless, that you do not seem to be somebody who needs to do everything or somebody who just realizes the correct way that a venture ought to be finished.

Satisfy Your End of the Job

Your managers have certain desires for you through your colleagues. Continuously take care of your responsibility as well as could be expected. Try not to search for the path of least resistance or ask a colleague to do an aspect of your responsibilities. Be helpful and make sure to look for development in everything you do.

Regard People's Time and Priorities

We most of the time work under tension and cut off times. Regard your collaborators' requirement for focus. In the event that you have to interfere with them, ask first "Is it a decent time?" your solicitation is critical. Apologize for the interference and keep your solicitation brief. Recollect that every one of us has an alternate style of working, so regard your collaborators' style of time the executives and organizing their outstanding task at hand.

Be Eager to Admit Your Mistakes and Apologize Gracefully

Missteps occur. We do not purposefully make them. Concede when you are off-base or have committed an error and continue ahead with your work.

Put resources into Other Parts of Your Life.

Ensure that you are dealing with you and that your non-work life is advancing. Enjoy side interests, sports, and work out, travel, or mingling. Do whatever it takes not to take your work issues home. Change out of your work garments and your work attitude. Accomplish something altogether unique when you return home. Zero in on your family, your leisure activities, and yourself. This will invigorate you, helping you give everything during the following workday.

Comprehend That Life would not Always Be Perfect

You will have associates, supervisors, and managers that you generally like or concur with. When you find that you cannot work with specific people, at that point, it is an ideal opportunity to search for another work. By rehearsing the standards delineated here, you can figure out how to function effectively with troublesome people and thrive expertly simultaneously.

4.4 Understand Your Co-workers Action

In every workplace, you will encounter some difficult co-workers, and have to deal with some difficult situations at work is challenging because you have to meet them every day, yet rewarding, as it can teach you many interpersonal skills that will help you at work and everywhere else. So here is the deal, if a co-worker is difficult but does not affect your work, then you should ignore them. If you have to face them, then deal with them on a daily basis and it is known how to resolve the issue, then it is time for a change to take action. Here are given some tips on how to deal with difficult co-workers and resolve conflicts in your workplace that arise from your interactions with them:

Be Positive

Inspiration is infectious and no one needs to be around a Debbie Downer. On the off chance that you are consistently under stress as a result of a troublesome colleagues who is continually cutting you down, the nature of your work will be influenced. Regardless of whether the current circumstance is troublesome, it would help if you zeroed in on the encouraging points in your work. Be careful about over grumbling to others as you may appear to be a grumbler. Steady griping can fall off to others as you being amateur or lacking social aptitude, and high- ups may reprimand you for other office hardships. There might be a silver lining as you struggle to beg positive. Inquire as to whether there is something in particular about this individual you can appreciate.

When Required, Make a Move

Making a move does not mean calling your colleague out or threatening them. Commonly, your colleague does not understand that they are troublesome. Make a move in non-angry ways. Pull the individual aside in private and reveal to them how you feel. Utilize your relational abilities to work it out. Tell them that you are endeavoring to have a positive workplace, making a move as such might conceivably work and help change their official conduct.

In the event that unpretentious activities like this are not working and you are managing an office menace, you presumably need to make a move promptly to prevent the circumstance from deteriorating. Let your associate realize that their conduct is hostile or troublesome and that you are eager to bring it up if essentially. Whatever choice you make, be confident about it. The more drawn out this issue goes on, the more your work and individual life will endure. Manage the move when you are genuinely steady.

View from Above

Work is not some place for a show. It is the place you ought to be going to complete your work and spotlights on the main job. As expressed previously, you consistently stay in charge of your feelings. Dodge all youthful responses that will just reflect adversely back onto you. Try not to prattle, waste talk, or leave negative notes around the workplace. Remain quiet, cool and gathered consistently to show that you are the greater individual in the event that you let your troublesome colleague get to you. At that point you will endure considerably more negative results. Discover approaches to abstain from connecting with them.

Take advantage of the circumstances

You might be close to your colleagues, and attempt to capitalize on the tight spot and gain from it. Utilize your delicate aptitude and conversational methods to discover more about their perspective and to attempt to get better than what they are used to. Ideally, you will have the option to see what they are accustomed to, and this will make working with them simpler later on.

With regards to troublesome colleagues, we would not have the option to turn them off or nullify them. However, we can generally utilize our relational abilities to manage office issues in a controlled way. Living as indicated by the cardinal excellence gives us a controlling structure.

Here, we recommend numerous manners by which Stoicism can assist you with adapting and flourishing at work. It can assist you in adapting to temporariness and change. The cutting edge of work is described by constant and exponential change, fueled by mechanical advances. The present professions would not work tomorrow; a large number of yesterday's 'hard' aptitudes are now obsoleted, with 'human abilities,' for example, flexibility and versatility center to progress. These are the very abilities that Stoicism teaches.

As opposed to opposing change, stoics acknowledge that it is characteristic and vital, and that outside component is not inside our control. When the change is negative stoics encourage that we experience only our powerlessness to acknowledge the change. Apathy encourages us to conquer obstructions, uneasiness and stress. We can control functions and circumstances, yet we can control how we respond to them regarding our contemplations and activities. Recall that Stoicism is not tied in with stifling our feelings yet changing them by sending how they are associated with our convictions and perspectives.

Practice negative visualization as it includes offering thought to what things you esteem the most in your life and afterward envisioning to lose those things. Not just does this help us to acknowledge what we have today, it can likewise be utilized as the apathetic rendition of pre-mortem arranging, setting up for most pessimistic scenarios and empowering us to dodge them, at times. Mishaps weigh most intently on the people who anticipate only favorable luck.

There is an intelligence in observing the glass half unfilled - and a considerable amount of humor as well. Aloofness urges us to complete things. Apathy fabricates mindfulness, passionate knowledge, and fearlessness. It is at the center of the Stoic way of thinking, which, thus, is vital to flourishing in the cutting-edge working environment. The Stoics were pioneers of getting zero in on what today is. To construct Stoicism we should look inwards, assuming the ability to do activities, while testing twisted intuition with discerning methodology; for instance, moving from "I did not win the pitch; I am a disappointment" and "the pitch turned out poorly to " I have won numerous others and can improve my strategy.

Marcus Aurelius advocated self-reflection and demonstrated it through journaling. Emotionlessness focuses on that certainty and confidence originates from inside as opposed to from outer approval and ought to be the products of carrying on with life as indicated by an ethical structure. Be your own onlooker; look for your own praise.

Chapter 5: Discover Peace in Between Yourself

We are regularly in strife with ourselves. We are not generally content with ourselves. When we think they have violated us, we get angry with others, manhandled us, harmed us, offended us, taken from us, or accomplished something that they should not have. At the point, when we think this way, we are not content with ourselves. In the end, when we are not content with ourselves, we blow up, and we fight back, occupy ourselves with diversion or occasions, or resort to drinking to overlook our difficulties.

When things seem to work for the time being, they acquire us despondency the long haul. Accordingly, any social connection can upset our genuine feelings of serenity. At times we are in strife with ourselves since we feel that we accomplished something we should not have or did not do what we ought to have.

We are accustomed to living with a somewhat upset mood more often. It appears to us to be the typical human condition. We do not understand that we could be more joyful.

Finding inward harmony in the advanced world is a noteworthy test. Everything about the present-day society feels like an impediment to encountering true serenity. In any case, there are approaches to discover and keep up internal harmony. So, when you work for 8 hours for five days every week, you have to discover equalization and keep your rational soundness flawless.

Internal harmony is a decision, and a significant number of your propensities decide how much harmony you have in your everyday life. Equalization is not just a thing you should accomplish; however, it should turn into a way of life. Concentrate on things you can control. Why stress over those things you cannot control? It sours your disposition and makes you less skilled. In a real sense, ask yourself, "Is this something I can control? Will stressing be gainful in any capacity? As a person, you need to know which things are inside your control. Anything past that can occupy you and put pressure on your life.

5.1 Invest Your Energy in Nature

The past generations did not live in a 3-room farm and eat microwave popcorn. Go for a long stroll in the recreation center or go through the end of the week outdoors. You will feel significantly extraordinary contrasted with sitting in a structure 24 hours consistently. There is something serene about investing energy among the fowls and the trees. Reflection is quieting. Reflection causes you to see life and its difficulties all the more precisely. Things are regularly in a way that is better than they appear. Contemplation can keep your psyche from exacerbating things than it truly is. It appears that what you are doing is worrying your twilight of working, stopping and pondering for a couple of seconds, and seeing the distinction it never really minds a while later.

5.2 Boost Your Confidence but Always for Possible Things

Be open and forward with your requirements and wants. You are not just bound to get what you need, yet you will likewise feel more in charge of your life — being latent outcomes in having less control, which contradicts internal harmony. Be striking without being forceful. Try not to let others hold you up. Take full charge of your life. You are in charge. Always try to boost your confidence but, remember to know the difference between chasing the impossible from possible.

5.3 Find Peace in Everyday Life

Whenever you are angered, you do not have to run away from these feelings. You do not necessarily have to go to some resort. You need to look inside.

No place is more peaceful than your own soul. Retreat there and remember the basic principle of differentiating things you can control and things you cannot. Forgiveness is under your control. Not caring about people's opinions is under your control.

5.4 Do not Be a Source of Your Own Problems

We are the wellspring of the greater part of our issues. It might be challenging to accept that the greatest hindrance to our not finding a sense of contentment with ourselves is not others, or conditions, or what befalls us. A large portion of our issues originate from us, and we can end them. Your most prominent trouble is in yourself. You are your own greatest article. You are favoring the correct course as opposed to following it. You see where genuine satisfaction lies. However, you do not have the mental fortitude to achieve it.

When we retreat into ourselves and consider how our reasoning makes our issues, how another person in a similar circumstance would not be irritated by it, why what's going on outside cannot be the reason for our issues, we will start to understand that we are the wellspring of our issues. On the off chance that we make our own issues, we can comprehend them also.

5.5 Our Absence of Certainty Upsets our Significant Serenity

We accept that our significant serenity is upset by our circumstances and the individuals we need to manage. We property our absence of certainty to something outside of us: others and our conditions. It is our inward absence of certainty that has made the external troubles with individuals and conditions. Our absence of certainty does not originate from trouble; the trouble originates from our absence of certainty. At the point when you retreat into your brain and placidly audit things, you will see that your psyche is not influenced regardless. In any event, when the body is beaten, the brain is not.

Affliction is an issue for the body, not the brain, except if the psyche concludes that it is. Suppose we put forth an attempt to put our upsetting considerations heavily influenced by our brain. In that case, we will discover bliss and harmony in our regular day to day existence, and our undesirable enduring will stop. In any case, as long as we permit ourselves to be constrained by our upsetting considerations, we will generally encounter issues and languishing.

This is the error we make. We permit our brain to constrain the internal adversary; we offer the triumph to the upsetting considerations.

On the off chance that we need genuine feelings of serenity in our regular day to day existence, at that point regardless of whether we cannot deny ourselves and single-distinctly appreciate other conscious creatures, on the off chance that we cannot change that much, in any event, we should rehearse poise, understanding that we and other aware creatures are actually equivalent in not craving even the smallest uneasiness and not being glad and fulfilled. In this, we are actually equivalent.

5.6 Change Your Mentality

We cannot work on trading ourselves for other people—denying ourselves and totally loving other conscious creatures—we ought to, at any rate, attempt to rehearse poise. Subsequently, the main thing we need to do in our regular daily existence is to change our mentality and, when you have an adversary, practice persistence with that individual. At the point when someone upsets you, you need to accept that and open the door to rehearse persistence. We need to produce composure, revoking ourselves and treasuring others, by thinking about the generosity of others and the inadequacies of self-valuing. At any rate, we need to rehearse composure. So, you can see that building up a decent heart is the absolute first thing we have to do.

Regardless of how much riches and material we have aggregated, regardless of how long we have examined, regardless of how great our notoriety, regardless of the number of individuals we have underneath us, working for us, on the off chance that we do not rehearse tolerance and the great heart we will have no true serenity by any stretch of the imagination. Regardless of whether we have a large number of dollars in houses everywhere in the world, as long as we have not managed to value the mind, we will have no genuine feelings of serenity.

The individual who upsets us is the person who offers us true serenity. By rehearsing tolerance and creating adoring generosity and empathy for this individual, our resentment lessens. Step by step, we think that it is increasingly hard to blow up, and when we do, it goes on for more limited and more limited timeframes. Companions and partners do not offer us the chance to rehearse persistence, adoring graciousness, and empathy. We need to depend on foes for that.

5.7 Remember Whose Opinion Matters

Take a couple of moments to make a rundown of whose endorsement is essential to you. At that point, get some information about the cause of that want. How might you offer yourself what you want from others? Figure out how to source endorsement from inside instead of seeking after it from the individuals throughout your life. While drinking in acclaim from others is sustaining, depending on it as successive food may leave you hungry for additional.

Rundown your accomplishments. They can be little, for example, figuring out how to ride a bicycle or make your bed — or enormous, for example, graduating from school, continuing sound connections, or voyaging abroad without anyone else. Consider the means it took for you to accomplish your victories.

Have a composed or spoken discussion with those dreadful voices that demand you will never have what you need. State what you need to communicate with fearlessness and assurance. Envision achieving your objectives. Make it a full tangible encounter. How can it look, feel, smell, taste, and hear to have what you need? Rehash until this perception feels instilled.

Assume acknowledgment of your accomplishments. Thank individuals who praise you instead of instinctually redirecting. Work on gloating. Recognize at any rate one ability daily. Radiate certainty, in any event, when you do not feel it. Exemplify the inclination you need to have.

At the point when you get productive analysis, see the truth about it: redirection, not slamming. In the event that the input is conveyed brutally or with the plan to abuse power, consider it to be an occasion to reexamine. Make or join a care group in which you share your triumphs and difficulties. Discover responsibility accomplices with whom you can check inconsistently.

5.8 Do not Think You can Do anything You Want

If you just set your attention to it. That is a typical thing a few people like to tell kids, right? You can do anything you want. You just set your attention to it. You cannot do all that you like to do. You cannot be taller or shorter. It is alright. It is simply something you cannot do, regardless of the amount you may need to.

This seeps into more subtle zones throughout your life. So, recollect this about yourself, that you are human, as well, and that you cannot do all that you like to do. Also, while this might be baffling now and again, it is actually a blessing, these restrictions. Luxuriate in the restrictions you have been given, and use them as consent to being magnificent in your qualities. Relish the things you can do, and do not perspire the things you cannot.

5.9 Do not Suffer Imagined Troubles

You are tormented by any outside thing. It is not this thing that upsets you, yet your own judgment about it. Furthermore, it is in your capacity to clear out this judgment now. You are upset not by what occurs but rather by your assessment of it. That is an exemplary Stoic guideline. Your distraught soul originates from making a decision about an external function as unfortunate or awful.

You trouble yourself regularly through crying, groaning, and grumbling about it. Remember that: nothing; however, assessment is the reason for a distraught soul. Mischief does not originate from what occurs—an irritating individual or disliked circumstance—however, from your response to it. Your mischief originates from your conviction about the function. So, when somebody presses your catches, it is not this individual, but rather the translation that harms you.

It's your supposition that powers the negative emotions. Your response chooses whether mischief has happened or not. Marcus Aurelius says that it should be like this in light of the fact that in any case, others would have control over you. What's more, that is not known to mankind's expectation. Just you approach your psyche, no one, but you can destroy your life.

Assume liability. Else, I could compose here that you are a snap, and you would be hurt regardless. Yet, I try not to have this control over you. In the event that you get injured by my words, at that point, it is your translation, not my words, that hurt you. It is insane looking at this logically: The understanding of comment has such a monstrous force. It is the distinction between a face secured by a grin or doused in tears.

You fundamentally have the ability to get filled by verbally abusing. In the event that you decipher these words in a positive manner, at that point, you draw power from them. It is your judgment that harms you. Also, it is your judgment that engages you. I recall some soccer star saying something along the lines of, "The whistling and booing by the restricting fans at whatever point I have the ball, that spurs me."

While another player may get injured and loses center, this one gets energized by it. Presently whenever you're upset by something, recollect that is your judgment about the circumstance that harms you. Attempt to eliminate the judgment, and the hurt will evaporate, as well. Try not to pass judgment on the function as fortunate or unfortunate. Simply take it for what it is worth — and you would not get hurt.

It is your response that shows whether you have been hurt or, on the other hand, not. As Marcus Aurelius puts it: "Decide not to be hurt — and you would not feel hurt. Try not to feel hurt — also, you have not been." It is clearly problematic, yet it's acceptable to know nonetheless. Simply attempt this: Do not whimper, groan, or gripe.

5.10 Try not to Abandon People nor Yourself

As you push ahead along the way of reason, individuals will hinder you. They will always be unable to shield you from doing what's sound, so do not let them take out your generosity for them. Keep a constant watch on the two fronts for very much based decisions and activities yet in addition to tenderness with the individuals who might impede our way or make different challenges. For blowing up is likewise a shortcoming, the same amount of as deserting the undertaking or giving up under frenzy. For doing either are an equivalent departure—the one by contracting back and the other by alienation from family and companion.

You should learn groundbreaking thoughts and various approaches to approach and get things done. You set up as a regular occurrence what impacts you the most, and as an outcome, you dump your old conduct and introduce the recently learned. The fact of the matter is, you change after some time. You do not adhere to old propensities since it is helpful. You need to develop and attempt new ways and keep those that work. As you push ahead along the path of reason," Marcus says, "individuals will hold you up." When you are putting in new propensities and attempt to gain ground, others probably would not be as speedy or, in any event, ready to track.

Presently, it is our test not to forsake our new way and, simultaneously, not to relinquish our loved ones. You should not forsake your new way practically in light of the fact that others may object to it. You should not relinquish those different people, either. Do not just discount them or leave them in the residue. Try not to get distraught or battle with them. All things considered; they are at a similar spot you were in the no so distant past. We should not relinquish others since we decided to change, yet we likewise should not surrender our new way. That is a test we will all face with different thoughts and qualities.

Eating less (or no) meat, burning through less time playing computer games, observing less news, investing more energy outside, understanding more, purchasing less material stuff, working out more frequently, halting hitting the bottle hard consistently, or griping less. Presently it is an intense test to adhere to your new way and not to surrender others. Since the distinctions may be gigantic. However, you attempt and give it some time. Show others your reasons, and possibly bargain once every month. Stay kind and patient with others. All things considered; you were at a similar spot in the relatively recent past. Discover approaches to adhere to your new way. Try not to twist your qualities.

5.11 Schedule Stillness in Your Life

Today, quietness can be challenging to find. Such an uproar both inside and outside our minds. Countless errands on our daily agendas. In any event, a few screens close enough. Yet, tranquility is as yet conceivable. It, as well, is inside our span at whatever point we need it. You can develop tranquility while strolling on a bustling road, while mayhem twirls surrounding you. Some of the coolest encounters are to be in the busiest of spots and to cultivate an inward and outside quietness for yourself.

The key is to make a goal of tranquility — to have some purposefulness about how we are conveying ourselves in a given second — and to zero in on what is inside our control. For example, you may genuinely back off by sitting, gradually strolling, or in any event, resting. You may diminish outside upgrades in your current circumstance by bringing down the lights and turning down the music.

Tranquility is amazing. Being still resembles renewing the stores. It permits us existence. It gives us reality to self-reflect and really hears our musings. It additionally calms our sensory system. Stillness produces the counter-pressure fix by permitting us some chill time without absolutely looking at and being numb to our experience. Quietness appears to be unique at various minutes and in various circumstances.

Here are a few bits of knowledge and recommendations on rehearsing quietness:

Relax. Taking moderate and full breaths actuates the parasympathetic framework and eases back your pulse. Practice when you need it. Schedule your quietness. When you are not making quietness precipitously, plan it, keeping this time-hallowed. Or on the other hand, set a caution on your telephone. Focus on it and let others know in your life, so they can respect this time you are saving for yourself.

Locate a most loved spot. Once more, you can encounter tranquility at anyplace. Be that as it may, it can assist with beginning at most loved spots. This may be outside, for example, a recreation center or seat, or at home, in complete quietness. Tune in to delicate music. Now and again, individuals fear being separated from everyone else with their considerations. This is while making more structure is useful. One route is by tuning in to delicate, slow music. Music likewise is incredible when quiet gets stunning.

Continue quieting phrases. This additionally gives your quietness structure. You can have extra instances of tranquility: guiding musings to serene proclamations; zeroing in on an alleviating picture that inspires a feeling of quietness, for example, a characteristic scene; going for a moderate stroll without talking or tuning in to music;

plunking down and taking full breaths until you feel tranquility in your body; shutting your eyes for a few minutes; journaling; or perusing. Recollect that our general surroundings in all mayhem do not mean we generally need to join in. Inside you, there is tranquility and asylum to which you can withdraw at any time.

5.12 Buy Tranquility at Low Price

Beginning with things of little worth—a touch of spilled oil, a little taken wine—rehash to yourself: 'For such a little value, I purchase quietness and significant serenity.' Saud Epictetus. This is one of the top Stoic thoughts. "I purchase peacefulness." This sentence spared you on many occasions from blowing up and bothered. How frequently do we blow up at trifles? How regularly do we lose our brains for something irrelevant? We let little things excite our outrage, and our noteworthy activities stir outrage in others, etc.

The Stoics need to remain quiet even amidst a tempest, but then we go insane when our roomie neglects to do the dishes, abandons slide marks in the latrine, or does not do his errands. It clearly should not be like this. Before you respond to whatever excites outrage inside, state to yourself: "I buy peacefulness." Then grin, do the main priority and proceed onward with your life. Nothing occurred. You will, before long, understand that the little things that typically disturb you are not worth the issue. Simply swallow whatever sentiments emerge inside and proceed onward. This will spare you a huge load of nerves and energy.

The primary test is this: we should know about the emerging sentiments in any case. So, we should have the option to step in the middle of boost and programmed reaction. Furthermore, when we are in that hole, we have to have the self-restraint to really purchase quietness and not respond by any means. The more frequently you are ready to purchase serenity, the simpler it will get. What's more, you will become ready to try and purchase quietness in additionally testing circumstances. Slip marks are simple. It just takes a couple of moments to tidy up.

The fact is, the more you work on purchasing serenity, the better you will get. Eventually, this all comes down to the Stoic rule that it is not functions that make us furious, rather our judgment about those functions. When we perceive our capacity and bring enough mindfulness and control into testing circumstances, at that point, we are headed to turn into a genuinely tough and undaunted individual. That is simply the way you need to go. Ask yourself: "In which circumstances would I be able to purchase serenity all the more regularly?"

5.13 Love and Forgive People Who Stumble

At whatever point you meet somebody, state to yourself from the start, 'What are his presumptions concerning what is generally acceptable and awful throughout everyday life?' When somebody acts like your adversary, affronts, or contradicts you, recollect that he was just doing what appeared to him the correct thing, he did not have the foggiest idea about any better and let yourself know: 'It appeared so to him.

Stoicism calls for absolution. The Stoics help themselves to remember the obliviousness of the transgressors. They do not foul up deliberately, yet what they do is by all accounts the correct thing in their circumstances. It is our unique benefit to adore even the individuals who stagger. He helps himself to remember four things: (1) that the staggering individuals are family members, (2) they foul up automatically, (3) we will all be dead soon in any case, and (4) we must be hurt. Accordingly, it is inside our capacity (and obligation) to cherish even the individuals who stagger.

Present exoneration for some things; look for pardon for none. Others do what appears consistent with them, and, along these lines, he openly absolves them. Also, simultaneously he realizes that they do not excuse him. This is on the grounds that it does not appear to be important to them. Be excusing, regardless of whether others are not. You show others how it is done, realizing that they do not perceive what you see.

It might be said, the Stoics see staggering individuals as misinformed and ailing in astuteness, more like youngsters than malignant individuals. They neglect to perceive that what they are doing is not even for their own wellbeing. They are incognizant with regards to see. It resembles a sickness. They do not perceive what they are doing. Furthermore, on the grounds that they are sick, disliking them would not help anyone So, why should we accuse them? We should not hate what they do on the grounds that resemble detesting their disease. The main proper reaction is sympathy and absolution.

Marcus makes a perfect examination: He says wanting for the unconscious man not to foul up resembles wanting for a fig tree not to deliver figs, infants not to cry, and ponies not to neigh. These are unavoidable things. They simply occur commonly. Try not to want for individuals not to foul up, rather wish for the solidarity to be open-minded and excusing.

5.14 Remember Your Good fortune

Do no set your brain on things you do not have as though they were yours; however, remember the good fortune you really have and figure the amount you would want them on the off chance that they were not at that point yours. Yet, be careful, that you do not esteem these things to the point of being a pain in the event that you ought to lose them." Since we overlook how great things we really have and how kind of life has been with us before. Remember to be appreciative of what you have—even notwithstanding affliction.

Marcus helps us here to remember three things: Material things are not significant, do not accumulate and store that stuff. Be thankful for all you have. Be mindful so as not to get connected to those things. Who cares what others have? You can choose for yourself what's really significant and what is not—zero in on yourself. Perceive how life has been liberal with you. You need not bother with increasingly more stuff. You need less. What's more, you will be more liberated. The more you have, the more you can lose.

Be appreciative of what you have. Value those things. Also, discover approaches to exploit what you as of now have. Here's a heavenly law Epictetus liberally shares with us: "And what is the perfect law? To keep a man's own, not to guarantee what has a place with others, but rather to utilize what is given, and when it is not offered, not to want it; and when a thing is removed, to surrender it promptly and quickly, and to be grateful for the time that a man has had its utilization. Desire not what you do not have, but rather acknowledge what you do have.

Continuously be prepared to give back what you have been given, and be appreciative for the time it was yours to utilize—what a straightforward law. We should tattoo that into our psyches. The best gifts of humankind are inside us. A savvy man is content with his parcel, whatever it might be, without waiting for what he has not. Let's keep such a disposition of appreciation consistently for all that we have and for all that comes in our direction. Make a point to be thankful consistently. The most effortless approach to do that is to record a couple of explicit things you are appreciative of every day. Add that to your morning schedule when you state Marcus' words that say when you emerge in the first part of the day, consider what a valuable benefit it is to be alive—to inhale, to think, to appreciate, and to adore. Remember not to stick to those things. They are just obtained from nature and can be removed at a snap.

5.15 Discovering Peace by Releasing Regrets

It is both enlightening and profitable for us to recall that the demonstration of delivering lament is more about broadening affection and empathy into any outstanding spots of agony. It is less about who or what ought to be accused or disgraced for the first injuring. We, as a whole, commit errors. It is an inescapable, yet trivial, result of being human. In the ideal situation, we gain from them and let them go. Looking back botches regularly show us what did not work and what we could improve next time.

Certain errors, notwithstanding, particularly ones that we consider to be uncalled-for and terrible, will wait in our recollections, regularly making a continuous, ever-developing great of passionate agony. Regardless of whether this agony is coordinated towards oneself or toward another, it contributes essentially to pressure, misery, and medical affliction.

Second thoughts that we consider hard to deliver come in all shapes and sizes. They keep on negatively affecting our lives. A few second thoughts revolve around horrendous encounters. Different second thoughts bring about sentiments of unfairness about things that we did, that we wish we had not done or things that we didn't do that we wish we had done.

Hatred is a sand trap. As we persistently replay past pernicious functions in our psyches, we sink further into an interior climate of heightening pressure, exhaustion, and disengagement. Moving from feeling severe to feeling better will include the hallowed work of recognizing, approving, lamenting, and delivering past pain. Describing and naming the profound misfortunes related to our second thoughts and the numerous agonizing outcomes we have encountered accordingly will serve to start to open and deplete the inner overabundance of enthusiastic agony. Thinking about ourselves in this manner will encourage us in arousing our inside assets of nurturance and self-comprehension.

Proactively welcome rationality of heart and brain by harping on quiet pictures. At the point when your musings and feelings re-visitation pictures of past agony, tenderly divert your concentration to quieting pictures of consolation, break, and alleviation. In the mending cycle, what we put in is frequently, in reality, more significant than what we take out. Start to extricate the hold of enduring by ardently advising yourself that you merit harmony rather than more torment.

Chapter 6: Become a Modern Stoic

Modern Stoicism can be described as an academic and well-known development that started towards the twentieth century. It is not to be mistaken for Neo-stoicism, a closely resembling wonder in the seventeenth century. The expression "Modern Stoicism" covers both the restoration of enthusiasm for the Stoic way of thinking and the philosophical endeavors to change Ancient Stoicism to the modern world's language and calculated structure. The ascent of Modern Stoicism had gotten consideration in the global media since around November 2012 when the primary Annual Stoic Week function was organized.

Stoicism is something beyond an allowance of faith-based expectations or practices. It is a philosophy of a specific time and spot. Be that as it may, Modern Stoicism, otherwise called the New Stoicism, has taken on a distinctly American feel. While the Stoics of the Classical time instructed that "uprightness is the main acceptable," New Stoics appear to zero in utilizing antiquated lessons to be more successful online media brand administrators.

The central point of interest is how we take a gander at Stoicism. We regularly peruse and hear that it is a down to earth theory, one that conveys a lot of fight tried techniques, practices, and activities that will lessen nervousness, sadness, increment bliss and in general permit us to lead better, additionally satisfying, carries on with regardless of the target difficulties and issues we face. A large number of us come to Stoicism when something troublesome occurs. We lose our employment. We experience extreme separation and build up a genuine sickness. This chapter will guide you on how to practice Stoicism in this modern world.

6.1 Who is a Modern Stoic?

Stoicism is a perpetual way of thinking and living life. Human instinct will consistently be human instinct, regardless of what culture or purpose of source it emerges from. Emotionlessness at its center spotlights the most proficient method to manage human instinct, notwithstanding encountering the inconceivability that life has to bring to the table. This is extremely engaging. The Stoics accept an assortment of things, yet a large portion is based on making a solid inner locus of control.

An inside locus of control is the point at which you have the conviction that you are answerable for your prosperity or disappointment in this world. You cannot utilize your youth, how you were raised, or things that transpired in the past as a reason for inactivity and casualty. Life can be summarized in one sentence: "Such and such occurred. So, what are you going to do about it?" What are you going to do about it today? What is your reaction to this test, presently?

From that ground zero, the modern Stoics had faith in gathering enough inspiration, enough force, enough energy to adjust to daily routine conditions and experience. Each individual is answerable for their activities on the planet and the energy they bring to various connections. The Stoics accepted this. Here are four territories that the modern Stoics zeroed in on seriously to help reinforce their inner locus of control in this modern world.

Facades

"What do we respect? Facades. What do we spend our energy on? Facades. Is anyone surprised, at that point that we are in dread and misery? By what others mean would it be able to be?" – Epictetus discourses.

"Facades" are what the Stoics call "any person or thing that is not you." Extended, this is essentially anything outside your own brain. Climate, legislative issues, others' activities, regardless of whether you land terminated from your position, affliction, even passing itself – are generally facades. The Stoics propose self-restraint, sound judgment, and separation to manage facades fundamentally the same as Buddhism.

The Stoic would incline toward for the climate to be radiant, governmental issues to have fellowship, never to become ill, and life to go to his direction – yet he is not excessively joined to whether they do or do not. This is a proactive way to deal with life because, as opposed to having self-sympathy and lost control, the Stoic asks himself: What is the best game-plan, and what would be an ideal next step?

Death

Whatever you are doing, or which era you have been living in, be aware of death. As stated, one of these facades is death. Death is unavoidable, yet it is something a great many people dread somehow. Hence, the Stoics see it under an extreme light, and it is one of the fundamental subjects of Stoic request. Indeed, in works like On the Shortness of Life, Seneca says that it takes a lifetime to figure out how to live and kick the bucket.

Figuring out how to live takes an entire life, and, which may amaze you more, it takes an entire life to figure out how to kick the bucket. Many of us do not utilize our time carefully, so we are caught off guard for death when it comes. Surprisingly, numerous people can, without much of a stretch, except that they are ensured to experience a decent life since they carry on with a long everyday routine. It is accurately this line of reasoning that keeps people from carrying quality to their activities.

There is no purpose behind you to think anybody has lived long because he has silver hair or wrinkles. He has not lived long. He has existed long. It is exceptionally simple to exist, occupy the room, and devour. It is hard to, in reality, to live. In present-day Stoicism, something like passing ought to be given close consideration. Death assumes no genuine function in any of our lives. Death is viewed as something theoretical and like something that "happens to others." This makes us not to fret about our days as they transform into weeks, months, and years.

It is truly conceivable to spend a whole lifetime in inertness and not achieving anything of significant worth essentially because we did not have the foggiest idea about our time. In all things, left us alone, careful, and let us carry characteristics to our activities as though it was our last day on earth.

Peace of Mind

In the entirety of life's conditions, the modern Stoics advocate for common sense and true serenity even notwithstanding overpowering trepidation. The primary objective is to utilize misfortune to fortify the will, something like putting signs on fire.

The objective of poise is to keep up a fair perspective that can change terrible circumstances into impartial or even great ones. For that, you will require focus and sober-mindedness, two characteristics that will assist you with getting to where you want to go. The following are given some practices to become a true modern stoic.

6.2 Self-awareness

When you see yourself plainly, you are more inventive. You settle on better choices, and assemble grounded connections. We are better specialists who get more advancements. Internal mindfulness tells how you see your own qualities, desires, interests, fit with your current circumstances, responses, and their effect on other people. Inner mindfulness is linked to higher work, relationship fulfillment, and individual control; it is identified with nervousness, stress, and sadness.

The subsequent classification, outer mindfulness teaches seeing how others see you. People who understand how others perceive them are more talented at demonstrating empathy and taking others' viewpoints. Self-mindfulness and self-awareness are squandered on the fact that it does not bring about self-acknowledgment. Mindfulness does not make everybody more joyful. It makes a few people more hopeless. Since supposing that extraordinary mindfulness is combined with self-judgment, at that point, you are only getting more mindful of the apparent multitude of ways you have the right to be judged.

Creating self-awareness and developing our propensities in associating with others is a long-lasting cycle, which ceaselessly requires taking some break and getting what the Stoics call "the view from above." Know yourself more. Understand who you are. When you know yourself better, it will become easy to handle whatever comes your way in life. You would have much more clarity of how things actually are.

6.3 Overcome Fear with Your Reason and Preparation

We are more scared than hurt, and we experience the ill effects of a creative mind than from the real world. What we dread will regularly not occur in all actuality. Yet, our nonexistent dread has genuine outcomes. We are kept down by our feelings of dread. We are deadened by what is not genuine. The Stoics think about the risk of dread. We are aimlessly attempting to forestall what we dread. The essential driver of the fear is the projection to the future about something we cannot control that causes a hazardous measure of stress.

We fear as we need what is out of our capacity, or we are excessively connected to something that is not in our capacity to keep. We are connected to people we love and dread losing them. We are appended to the security of ordinary compensation. What's more, we want what is not in our capacity to get. We should quit appending ourselves to outside things and wants, which are not heavily influenced by us. Since an absence of control prompts fear. He who does not want anything beyond his ability to do anything about cannot be restless.

It is so imperative to get ready for provoking circumstances to emerge. Foreseeing disasters is not tied in with demolishing the present, yet streamlining it. You will be less scared of things that may never occur. The Stoics think the best way to overcome fear is by envisioning what we dread as it will occur and looking at it in our psyche — until we can see it with separation. The normal method to manage your fear is to escape it and attempt to consider something else.

The best possible approach to manage your thought process is to do it judiciously, smoothly, and frequently — until it gets comfortable. You will get exhausted with what you once dreaded, and your concerns will vanish. By standing up to your feelings of fear, you lessen the pressure brought about by those apprehensions. Marcus has another method of managing fear: "Clear your mind and take a few steps back to get back some composure. What you are afraid of is frequently a result of your mind, not reality."

You are apprehensive about something not on the grounds that the truth of it is terrible, but since you figure out that reality would be awful. It all resembles a fantasy. That is the reason we should awaken and stop this. We are the ones keeping us down. See, you cannot fix every one of your feelings at the same time. Do your preparation and use your reason to get yourself out of those fears that hold you back.

6.4 Welcome the Discomforts

Nature has intermixed joy with fundamental things — not altogether that we should look for delight, but rather all together that the expansion of joy may make the vital methods for presence appealing to our eyes. Should it guarantee privileges of its own, it is an extravagance. Let us accordingly oppose these flaws when they are requesting passageway, on the grounds that it is simpler to deny them permission than to cause them to leave."

One practice the Stoics broadly stood was inviting a specific level of distress into their lives. They would leave certain joys for a period. They would inundate themselves in helpless climate conditions. They would shun wealth to not figure out how to stick to those things, or even purposely expose themselves to disparage. These practices were fairly in opposition to the Epicurean perspective on things, which was to eventually seek after delight. The Stoics knew, they were really unquestionably more substance and satisfied than their Epicurean friends.

To be Epicurean — one who essentially looks for the things in life that vibe the best — you need to actually be encountering delight. You are fundamentally living off consistent dopamine hits. In any case, those faculties get dulled inevitably, and you need greater and more unavoidable dosages ever to keep your pleasure sensors initiated at a similar level. When you begin running on the "gluttonous treadmill," genuine happiness turns out to be frustratingly subtle.

There are many explicit advantages of once in a while, inviting inconvenience and deliberately sacrificing some previous joys. It solidifies us to whatever disasters may come later on. The possibility of those incidents would not cause you nervousness since you realize you can withstand and even be content in pretty much any situation.

It encourages you to welcome the delights you do have when you have them. This is one of the practices most connected with Stoicism, and there are various explicit things you can do to invite uneasiness into your life and solidify your overall determination.

6.5 Affinity for others

Living is not made in seclusion. It is lived with different people. Thus, you must have an affinity for others who think uniquely in contrast to what you do. The Stoics accentuated public help and a day to day existence "in the group" yet all the while "above" it. This is summarized by Marcus Aurelius when he said that when you get up in the first part of the day, let yourself know: the people you will manage today will be interfering, selfish, self-important, untrustworthy, envious, and irritable.

They resemble this since they cannot tell great from evil. Yet, you have seen the magnificence of good, and the offensiveness of fiendishness, and have perceived that the miscreant has a nature identified with my own – not of similar blood and birth, but rather a similar brain, and having a portion of the celestial. To feel outraged at somebody, to walk out on him: these are unnatural."

The Stoic method of living is eventually focused on people. Empathy offers a structure for living a more amicable and profitable life. In case you are ready to consider Stoicism and apply its statutes, little will shake you off the center of whatever you are attempting to achieve in this brief timeframe of life.

6.6 Practice to Become Less Greedy

In our journey to turn into a decent person, we need to confront an intense foe called voracity. Greed is the perpetual craving to get an ever-increasing number of things throughout everyday life. Insatiability is the thing that directs our activities and musings in the event that we are not careful enough. It is insatiability that advises you to get that bigger part of the pie or that greater bunch of chips.

Insatiability is contemplating yourself more often than not, without thinking about what the other individual feels. Greed annihilates companionships, connections and is the main driver of greater humankind inconveniences like war and debasement. When you do not control and get mindful of it, your voracity will just increment as time passes. Also, regardless of whether you satisfy all your cravings, you would not have the option to carry on with an upbeat life since it is the idea of covetousness to want for another wish when one wish is satisfied.

Greed does not have any cutoff. When you think having that enormous house or a room brimming with cash will fulfill your voracity, you are off-base. Regardless of whether you get that, you will need a considerably greater house and more cash. Voracity is hazardous for you, yet for our entire human race and each life on this planet. The plants, creatures, and common assets we have here are restricted. When you do not control your eagerness, you will wind up pulverizing this lovely planet. It is just difficult to satisfy each individual's desire on this planet.

You can control your cravings and greed to live an upbeat, tranquil, and fulfilled life. It does not mean you need to keep low objectives throughout everyday life or kill your fantasies. It is just about understanding what you need and what you do not. However, before you beat greed, you need to comprehend it is the real essence. Why does it emerge in your psyche? What makes you need that greater bit of pie? Why do you act covetously over and over?

Greed needs an object of want, something you should have whenever you have seen it. This object of want can be anything – chocolate, drugs, contraptions, individual from another gender, or simply a bigger part of the pie.

Attempt a little test. Envision your object of want before you. It very well may be anything – pick one that implies the most to you. Envision how it would feel in the event that you had it at the present time? How might you devour it? How will you feel in the wake of devouring it? Presently as you are envisioning this, attempt to watch your psyche simultaneously – How your brain responds when it sees an alluring.

It is your brain that makes you covetous and compels you to play out those activities to satisfy your greed. The reason for this little analysis is to disclose to you that it is not your body that needs those things; it is your brain that makes you suspect as much. It is as straightforward as that. There is no riddle, no outside examination expected to demonstrate it. You can do this exploration all alone and become acquainted with firsthand how your psyche fools you into having those items. Furthermore, you can do this just by watching your psyche.

Controlling your brain is the way to control your greed. Thus, we should attempt to comprehend this cycle in detail. When you see your object of want before you, your eyes see it first. However, it is your psyche that perceives that object. When perceived, the psyche instructs you to have that object. And afterward, you make a move – like get that pie and eat it – to satisfy what your brain says.

You need to stay alert for any circumstances in which you act avariciously. At exactly that point, would you be able to conquer avarice? In this way, we should perceive how we can defeat covetousness with a model.

So, to become less greedy, you have to prevent yourself from acting, the moment an egotistical idea strikes a chord. So, when the idea to snatch an alluring item reaches your psyche, stop in that general area. Try not to make any move. Simply watch your psyche at that point. Simply observe what your brain is constraining you to do. Furthermore, when you become mindful that you are insatiable, let go of that thing, and rather pick the choice that does equity to others as well.

Again, when greed emerges, do this equivalent thing. Stop the moment when you understand you are ravenous, comprehend the greed inside you, release it, and afterward pick the choice that is best for everybody. When you practice this route for not many occasions, you will understand that you generally had the decision to pick among ravenousness and liberality. It is just that you never thought you had.

It will make you let go of your eagerness totally. Sure, it is preposterous to expect to give everything throughout everyday life. You will esteem a few belongings and encounters. Be that as it may, you will never do it at the expense of others' expense. Your life will turn out to be quieter, more joyful, and good when you surrender ravenousness in each part of your life. Be it companionship, connections, or people you have never met. You will need nothing from anybody. You will be on your way towards carrying on with a straightforward and significant life.

6.7 Shorten your expectation

A few things are inside our capacity, while others are definitely not. Inside our capacity are supposition, inspiration, wants, and repugnance. One of the mainstays of the Stoic way of thinking is not letting conditions beyond your ability to do anything to upset your balance. Such remotely directed conditions incorporate things you are accustomed to considering as being out of your hands, similar to the climate, traffic, and our wellbeing. Yet, it likewise incorporates things we regularly, wrongly accept we have control over, similar to the results of challenges and the achievement or disappointment of undertakings.

Perceiving that a lot of life is out of your control does not mean surrendering your feeling of office; rather, it implies zeroing in it on the main regions where you do have full control on your own activities. In this way, you will have fewer expectations and pain.

Rather than zeroing in on results — which are affected by outer conditions beyond your ability to do anything about — set objectives carefully identified with your own endeavors. Rather than defining an objective to dominate the game, make it an objective to get ready decently well, practice as hard as possible, and afterward play as well as could be expected. When you do those things and still lose, there is simply nothing more you might have done, so why fret?

Instead of defining an objective of landing the position or job you have applied for, make it your objective to get ready well, dress right, and answer each question decently well. When you do all that and do not land the position, it was not intended to be. When you set objectives, connect them to what you can control and what you cannot cut out of unrealistic expectations.

6.8 Stay Calm

These days, practically, we all wish that we could be more settled. It is one of the unmistakable longings of the cutting-edge age. Across history, people used to search out experience and energy. In any case, the greater part of us had all in all to a lot of that now. The longing to be quieter and the center is the new, always earnest need. A ton of disturbance is brought about by a ridiculous feeling of how surprising trouble is. We are abused by pointless pictures of the fact that it is so natural to accomplish and that it is so ordinary to succeed.

The narratives that authoritatively flow about what connections and vocations resemble tend lethally to minimize the more obscure real factors, leaving a large number of us upset, yet agitated that we are disturbed, feeling abused just as hopeless. We have to change our perspectives about what life resembles. We need – in the broadest sense – better workmanship, a sort that takes us all the more honestly into the real factors of connections and the working environment. We have to ensure we are encircled by precise contextual analyses of the customary agonies of everyday life. Not all that transpires happens regarding something about us. Our sentimental or expert disappointment does not need to be perused as retaliation for some wrongdoing we did.

To stay calm, we should decrease the heaviness of our unreasonable independence. Being too hopeful will not do any good for you. The desire that things will go well makes nervousness in light of the fact that, at some level, we realize that we cannot exactly rely on our expectations working out as intended. Furthermore, obviously, as things turn out, frequently they do not. We are on tenterhooks – and we endure. To reestablish our calmness, we have to turn out to be deliberately cynical. That is, to invest more energy, becoming accustomed to the genuine chance that things will work out rather severely.

A lot of plans fall flat; most things turn out badly; in any event, a large portion we had always wanted would work out. Cynicism hoses pointless and restless desires. It merits including that a skeptical perspective does not need to involve a day to day existence deprived of delight. Worriers can have a far more noteworthy limit with respect to gratefulness than positive thinkers, for they never anticipate that things should end up great thus might be stunned by the humble victories which infrequently break over their obscured skylines, thus giving you peace in the end.

You should not enable conditions to stir outrage. It resembles getting frantic at something far greater than you. It resembles thinking about something literally that could not care less about you. Things do not occur against us. They simply occur. Blowing up at a circumstance does not affect the circumstance. It does not transform or improve it. Intermittently, what maddens us does not generally hurt us, and our indignation will outlive the harm done to us. We are fools when we permit our serenity to be disturbed by trifles. That is the reason Marcus suggests pondering the fleetingness of our general surroundings.

What infuriates us presently will be overlooked tomorrow. Find a way to transform your outrage's signs into their contrary energies. Force yourself to loosen up your face, take a full breath, mollify your voice, and moderate your movement of strolling—your inward state will before long take after your outside, loosened upstate. You can likewise attempt to portray the circumstance driving you mad as impartially and unbiasedly as could reasonably be expected. This will save you time and assist you with seeing the circumstance with more prominent separation.

Also, we ought to consistently remember that it is not the circumstanced that hurt us, rather our translation about it. So, when somebody stirs your indignation, realize that it is actually your feeling energizing it. So, rather than being irate constantly and torture your life, remain calm and make yourself an individual to be adored by all and missed when you are no longer around.

6.9 You are not special

Things have consistently been the equivalent. People have been doing what they do. Certain perspectives and practices have traveled every specific way. However, people and lives have consistently been the equivalent—wedding, bringing up kids, becoming sick, kicking the bucket, battling, crying, snickering, devouring, imagining, protesting, beginning to look all starry eyed at, craving, and philosophizing—the same old thing. The things are equivalent to ten ages back and will be the equivalent in people in the future. Seneca, Marcus Aurelius, and Epictetus had similar battles as we have 2,000 years after. That is the reason their writings are still so significant today.

Marcus advises that everything continues repeating. Regardless of what occurs, remember this present: It is old news, from one apocalypse to the next. It fills the set of experiences books, old and current, and the urban areas, and the houses as well. The same old thing by any means." It is anything but difficult to accept that what's going on now is extraordinary. Yet, as tough people, we should oppose this idea and know that with a couple of exemptions, things are equivalent to they have generally been and consistently will be — the normal, worn-out things.

We are much the same as the people who preceded us. We simply have short visits until others simply like us will come when we are no more. The earth stands everlastingly. However, we will travel at different time and way. Before you pay attention to things as well, advise yourself that things that transpire are not uncommon. Hundreds have encountered it before you, and hundreds more will whenever you are gone. Sorry to let you know. However, you are not all extraordinary.

What befalls you is not so unique. How you carry on is not so exceptional. This may assist you in placing things in context. Furthermore, do not pay attention to everything. Furthermore, do not pay attention to yourself as well. It is normal. Likewise, this is another motivation behind why we should not be shocked at trifles — those things happen over and over; we should know about that. Things break, people bite the dust, games get lost, people fall flat—as the rose in spring and the natural products in summer—things will consistently repeat themselves.

Chapter 7: Find Real Happiness

This chapter will provide you an ideal opportunity to get to the core of Stoicism. What did these intriguing rationalists accept and instruct precisely? How could they intend to stay faithful to their obligation of a happy and content life? In what capacity can their standards set us up to confront whatever challenge life tosses at us? Furthermore, how might we tame our feelings and become an unflinching pinnacle of solidarity? It is straightforward. You have to go out in reality and train like a hero rationalist. On the whole, you have to realize the principles to play by, you have to recognize what to battle for, and you have to know which course to take.

These are the center standards of Stoicism that you will learn in this part. As also mentioned in the previous chapters in this book, this is the fundamental guarantee of the Stoic way of thinking. It is tied in with living an incredibly joyful and comfortable life. It is tied in with flourishing our lives. It implies to be at peace with yourself. Express your most elevated self in each second. We need to be on a proper footing with our most noteworthy self. We have to close the hole between what we are prepared to do and what we are really doing. This is genuinely about being your best form in the present time and place.

7.1 The Stoic Concept of Happiness

For the Stoics, the seed of our most noteworthy self is planted inside. We can carry on with an upright life—that is, a daily existence driven by reason and communicating our optimal self. This articulation shows noteworthy and admirable activities that advantage ourselves as well as other people. As mentioned in this book before, temperance is for all living creatures. It is about the flawlessness of their own tendency. Living happily is simply the flawlessness of communicating our most noteworthy self in each second. Keep in mind that living with righteousness, reason, and concurrence with nature are various articulations for a similar objective.

In the Stoic way of thinking, social activities are our obligations to other people. As level headed social animals, we ought to apply reason and express our most noteworthy selves to various fundamental everyday issues like our own psyche. As people with the capacity of sensible reasoning, we ought to consider our activities reasonably and admirably and consistently attempt to be as well as can be expected, with others. As social creatures who normally care for one another, we should try to live amicably with others and add to humanity's prosperity. As part of the vast universe, we should attempt to live amicably with nature, smoothly acknowledge functions that happen to us, and attempt to react admirably. This is why the Stoics utilized the Sage as an ideal because there are no ideal people.

The Stoic Triangle of Happiness

In Stoic triangle of happiness Eudaimonia depends upon three elements i.e. control, responsibility, and virtue.

Eudaimonia: It is a Greek word for prospering or life-fulfillment and encapsulates the ideal sort of satisfaction. It is the bliss one feels when they are on their deathbed, think back over their life, and comment, "I have carried on with a decent life!" To the Stoics, eudaimonia is an absolute satisfaction one could accomplish.

Control: The Stoic partitions the world into equal parts by a rule called the polarity of control. It says there are things in this world that we can control, similar to our judgment, motivation, wants, expectations. All else that lies outside our ability to control, similar to others' assessments of you, your body, notoriety, material belongings.

The Stoics encourage us to zero in on and improve at the things we control and let go of things we don't. The division of control causes us to whine less and keep up our composure more.

Responsibility: The Stoics approach us to assume liability for all transpiring, without accusing others. What great is accusing another? Since possibly they did it because of obliviousness, or they were under impulse or the best judgment they took around then. When we assume liability for things, including us, and conclude how to react to them with intelligence and judgment, it makes us more reasonable and autonomous — both liberating us from mental subjugation to other people.

Virtue: Righteousness is the foundation of Stoic bliss. The Stoics hold people carrying on with good for nothing day to day routines if they did not experience it with temperance. To accomplish eudaimonia, they carefully encourage us to rehearse the four cardinal ideals that could be expected.

The Stoic Love for Mankind

Act for the common welfare. We are social animals with a characteristic fondness toward others. Stoic way of thinking is loaded with goodness, tenderness, love for individuals, and regard for everyone's benefit, says Seneca. The objective is to be valuable, helping other people, and dealing with ourselves and every other person. The Stoics supported this thought that we ought to be worried about others, wish them to prosper, and build up a family relationship with the remainder of humanity. Treat even outsiders and the people who contradict us as family members — siblings and sisters, aunties, and uncles. We are all part of a similar world.

This common partiality frames the reason for shared love and companionship. An individual cannot accomplish anything extraordinary, says Epictetus, "except if he contributes some support of the network." That is the idea of the social and balanced creature we are. We are intended to live among other individuals, especially like honey bees. A honey bee cannot live alone. It perishes when separated." Marcus advantageously includes, "What carries no advantage to the hive carries none to the honey bee." Our activities must profit the normal government assistance, or they would not profit ourselves.

We are similar to a monstrous life form — all relying upon each other. Our social obligation is to feel a worry for all humanity, cooperate, and help one another. "For all that I do," says Marcus, "ought to be coordinated to this single end, the normal advantage and agreement." We cannot communicate our most noteworthy selves without simultaneously adding to the benefit of all. We look for the absolute best in ourselves. We will effectively think about the prosperity of all other individuals. The best for other people will be best for you. It is not so much that we are social as we like being around others. It is in the more profound sense that we were unable to exist without the assistance of others.

Subsequently, when we do great for other people, we really make our life happy and content. Profiting others is a type of righteousness, and it at last advantages ourselves as uprightness is its own prize. Since you know doing great to others benefits yourself, you could egotistically do great to others. It does not make a difference whether we do great to others for childish or unselfish reasons. Marcus says that satisfying your social obligations will basically give you the most obvious opportunity at having a decent and happy life. So, even Marcus Aurelius represented the benefit of all for a narrow-minded explanation—since he figured that it would give him the most obvious opportunity for a decent life.

Living with arête and guiding one's activities toward the benefit of everyone is its own prize. This is our inclination, and it is, at last, our most obvious opportunity to live a cheerful and easily streaming life. We should not look or wish for special rewards, for example, reverence from others since they are not inside our control and can blur rapidly. "Yet, the savvy individual can lose nothing," Seneca contends, "their own merchandise is held firm, bound in uprightness, which requires nothing from possibility, and in this way cannot be either expanded or decreased."

Your character, originating from your activities, is the thing that you can depend on consistently. In the Stoic way of thinking, it is sufficient to attempt to communicate your most elevated self consistently and direct your activities to everyone's benefit. That is everything you can do. Marcus Aurelius perfectly advises that a light sparkles until its fuel is completely spent. In that sense, we should light our lights of virtue and let them sparkle by communicating our most noteworthy variants; however long we may exist.

Accept Whatever Happens and Make the Best Out of It

Figure out how to apply your inclinations to the correct things as indicated by nature, and past that to isolate the things that exist in your capacity from those that do not. Some things are in our capacity, and others are most certainly not. The detachment between what is in our capacity and what is not is something we ought to consistently have prepared nearby, prepared to help us manage whatever life tosses at us. There are things which are up to us and things which are not; we ought to consistently "utilize what is in our capacity, and accept the rest as it occurs." This thought is the foundation of the Stoic way of thinking, and along these lines, assembles the path towards Stoic Happiness.

You remain inside and trust on a radiant day with some fortunate happenings. Out of nowhere, life turns into a passionate crazy ride — without you having a state in it. Giving capacity to things we have no immediate command over causes enthusiastic affliction. This is the reason the Stoics would advise us to assume control over and let ourselves choose when to get kicked around and not. The fact is, the Stoics need us to zero in on what we control and let the pugs mark where they may. What is it then that we have power over? We have discussed those things in detail in previous chapters.

We can choose what to intend for us and how we need to respond to them. We can decide to adjust what we do to goodness, as examined in the past part. We do not heavily influence all else. Our body, for instance, is not totally heavily influenced by us. We can definitely impact it with our conduct—we can lift loads, do some full-scale runs, and eat broccoli daily—yet this would not make our hips more modest, our shoulders more extensive, our nose straighter, or our eyes bluer. There are sure things that impact our bodies that we do not control.

Marcus Aurelius regularly helped himself to remember the influence he was allowed ordinarily—the ability to pick his activities and art his own character. He said people could not respect you for what's been conceded to you commonly. However, there are numerous different characteristics to develop. "So, show those excellencies which are completely in your own capacity—honesty, poise, difficult work, discipline, satisfaction, moderation, consideration, autonomy, effortlessness, tact, generosity." We are simply the main ones to prevent from developing these characteristics. It is inside our capacity to forestall violence, check our pomposity, quit longing for acclaim, and remain calm.

Focus on What You Can Control

This is the most conspicuous rule in Stoicism. Consistently, we have to zero in on the things we control and accept the rest as it occurs. What, as of now it must be acknowledged in light of the fact that it is past our capacity to fix it. What's past, our capacity is, at last, not significant for our thriving. What's significant for our thriving is the thing that we decide to do with the given outer conditions. So regardless of the circumstances, it is consistently inside our capacity to attempt to make the best with it and to live in agreement with our optimal self.

Accept Responsibility

Good and terrible come exclusively from yourself. You are answerable for your life on the grounds that each outside function you do not control, offers a territory you can control, specifically how you decide to react to that event. This is critical in Stoicism. They are not circumstances that make us hopeless or happy, rather our translation of those circumstances. This is the point at which a pinnacle of solidarity can be conceived — the second you choose to give outside functions no more control over you.

For the Stoics, happiness is determined by the way we react to different circumstances and what we think about them. Adjusting our activities to excellence is adequate for a cheerful and easily streaming life. Life disrupts the general flow. Reality raises itself before us. It gets us off guard, overpowering, causes dread, uncertainty, outrage, and sadness and makes us need to flee and cover-up. Things are harder than we suspected, and they happen uniquely in contrast to what we expected and wanted.

It just appears to be that life disrupts everything; in actuality, it is our negative feelings that disrupt everything. These extraordinary feelings vanquish our brain, really our entire being, make it difficult to think obviously, and encourage us to do something contrary to what we believe is correct. When our brain has been caught by negative feelings, or interests as the Stoics call them, for example, silly dread, distress, outrage, or covetousness, these interests dominate, and we respond hastily without having the option to consider it.

When the foe has entered the psyche, the reason is no more. It is either reason or enthusiasm; when energy is at the guiding wheel, the reason is tied up and choked in the storage compartment. So, the Stoics need us to conquer these nonsensical feelings of trepidation so that we can achieve genuine bliss.

Additionally, as a rule, these feelings are against our levelheaded nature as they disregard what is great. It is hasty and unreasonable to fear what is not perilous, it needs self-control for not conquering the inward opposition, and it is basically fainthearted. It is basic to defeat these negative feelings when you practice Stoicism. This is the reason a key aspect of the Stoic way of thinking is to forestall the beginning of negative feelings and to be set up to manage them successfully and not get overpowered in the event that they emerge, all things considered.

7.2 Definition of Happiness according to Ancient Stoics

These statements on life and joy by four of the most renowned Stoics will assist you with exploring genuinely and vivaciously through the questionable floods of life, with serenity, fortitude, and understanding.

Attempt to appreciate the extraordinary celebration of existence with other men! — Epictetus

Genuine bliss is about to live and appreciate our present, without on edge reliance upon the future, not to entertain ourselves with either expectations or fears; however, to rest happy with what we have, which is adequate, for he needs nothing. — Seneca

What you have appears to be deficient to you. At that point, however, you have the world, and you will yet be hopeless. — Seneca

Today I got away from nervousness. Or then again no, I disposed of it, since it was inside me, in my own observations — not outside. — Marcus Aurelius

Simply remember, the more we esteem things beyond our ability to do anything about, the less control we have. — Epictetus.

How long would you say you will stand by before you request the best for yourself and, in no example, sidestep the segregations of reason? You have been given the rules that you should support, and you have embraced them. What sort of educator, at that point, would you say you are as yet sitting tight for so as to allude your personal development to him? — Epictetus

There is just a single method to satisfaction, and that is to stop agonizing over things that are past the intensity of our will. — Seneca

Put aside a specific number of days during which you will be content with the scantiest and least expensive toll, with the coarse and unpleasant dress, saying to yourself the while, 'Is this the condition that I dreaded?' — Seneca.

It is outlandish that joy, and longing for what is absent, ought to actually be joined together. — Epictetus

One removes wealth from the savvy man; one leaves him still possessing all that is his: for he lives upbeat in the present and unafraid for what's to come. — Seneca

Conditions do not make the man. They just uncover him to himself. — Epictetus

A man might be called 'cheerful' who, on account of reason, has stopped either to trust or to fear: yet shakes likewise feel neither dread nor bitterness, nor do steers, yet nobody would call those things glad which can't fathom what joy is. — Seneca

Life is short and restless for the people who overlook the past, disregard the present, and dread what's to come. — Seneca

Nobody can be styled upbeat who has past the impact of truth: thus a cheerful life is unchangeable, and is established upon a valid and dependable insight; for the psyche is uncontaminated and liberated from all indecencies just when it can escape not only from wounds yet in addition from scratches when it will consistently have the option to keep up the position which it has taken up and safeguard it even against the irate attacks of Fortune. — Seneca

A mind-blowing bliss relies upon the nature of your musings. — Marcus Aurelius

Try not to look for everything to occur as you wish it would, but instead wish that everything occurs as it really will—at that point, your life will stream well. — Epictetus

You have control over your brain, not outside functions. Understand this, and you will discover quality. — Marcus Aurelius

If you need to get away from the things that badger you, what you're requiring is not to be in a better place, however, to be an alternate individual. — Seneca

What upsets people is not things themselves, however their decisions about these things. — Epictetus

That man is cheerful, whose reason prescribes to him the entire stance of his issues. — Seneca

No individual has the ability to have all that they need. However, it is in their capacity not to need what they do not have and to happily effectively utilize what they do have. — Seneca

You act like humans in all that you dread and like immortals in all that you want. — Seneca

How might one take from him that which is not his? So recall these two focuses: first, that everything is of like structure from never-ending and comes round again in its cycle, and that it connotes not whether a man will view very similar things for a hundred years or 200, or for the endlessness of time; second, that the longest-lived and the briefest lived man, when they come to pass on, lose the same thing very much. — Marcus Aurelius

Start without a moment's delay to live, and consider each different day a different life. — Seneca

It never stops to flabbergast me: we as a whole love ourselves more than others; however, care more about their sentiment than our own. — Marcus Aurelius

Next to no is expected to satisfy a daily existence; it is now inside yourself, your perspective. — Marcus Aurelius

7.3 Marcus Aurelius' Way of Finding Happiness

Here are some significant takeaways from the Roman Emperor's masterpiece.

Your own joy is up to You

Life's joy, Aurelius, stated, "relies on the nature of your considerations." The essence of his way of thinking is the idea that while we cannot control what befalls us, we can control our responses to the functions of our lives - and this invigorates a massive opportunity.

It is more difficult than one might expect. Indeed, however, Aurelius' own life is a positive confirmation of this saying. The ruler confronted extraordinary battles for an amazing duration, and his rule was damaged by close consistent fighting and sickness. His siblings and guardians likewise passed on at a young age.

Aurelius figured out how to live inside his spirit - or "inward bastion," as he put it - a position of harmony and serenity. Living from this space, he accepted, gave him the opportunity to shape his own life by controlling his considerations.

Life may not Give You what You Want. However, it will give You what You Need

Aurelius acknowledged that preliminaries and demands were an unavoidable piece of life, yet his conviction that life and the universe were generally acceptable, helped him to acknowledge the extreme stuff. The contention goes this way. Because life all in all is in the same class as it very well may be, the pieces of life are tantamount to they can be, so we should adore, or if nothing else acknowledges, all aspects of life.

However, Aurelius made it even one stride further, contending that hindrances are really our most prominent open doors for development and progression. They constrain us to rethink our way, locate another way, and eventually engage ourselves by rehearsing ideas like persistence, liberality, and boldness.

"The hindrance to activity propels activity," he composed. "What disrupts the general flow turns into the way."

Accept People the Way They are

Aurelius is not communicating blind confidence when he encourages people to discover shared views with others and look for the positive qualities in each individual they experience. In legislative issues and life, Aurelius had encountered how people could be egotistical and destructive to other people - he survived wars and uprisings - but then, he decided not to let the activities of others get to him. All things considered, he generally recollected that there was a portion of the "divine" in every one of us.

Aurelius accepted that all men are made to help out each other, similar to the "columns of the upper and lower teeth."

Genuine Harmony Originates from the Inside

We live rushed and high-octane lives. We may fantasize about moving endlessly from everything by going on a contemplation retreat or putting a hold on work to travel. However, as Aurelius unequivocally accepted, you do not have to get away from your current circumstance to discover a feeling of quiet. We can get to peacefulness any time as far as we could tell.

"People search for a retreat for themselves, by the coast, or mountains," Aurelius composed. "There is no place that a man can locate a more tranquil and inconvenience free retreat than as far as he could tell ... So continually give yourself this retreat, and recharge yourself."

Taking a "psychological retreat" through a reflection practice - or basically by bringing more care into your day - has been connected to emotional wellness benefits. Reflection has appeared to improve memory and consideration, lower feelings of anxiety, and upgrade passionate prosperity.

Treat Life as an Old and Steadfast Companion

Maybe the most noteworthy section of Meditations urges us to see life as being, in the expressions of the artist Rumi, "fixed in [our] favor." It is an incredible method of reevaluating any snag we experience. Aurelius said.

Genuine comprehension is to see the functions of life thusly. You are here for someone else's welfare. Everything is made advantageous for one when he welcomes a circumstance like this. Whatever emerges in life is the correct material to achieve your development and the development of everyone around you. This, in a word, is workmanship - and this craftsmanship called 'life' is a training appropriate to the two men and divine beings. Everything contains some unique reason and a shrouded favoring. What at that point could be odd or burdensome when all of life is here to welcome you like an old and steadfast companion?

Do not carry on as though you are bound to live until the end of time. What is destined looms over you? keep in mind that you can become great at this point." – Marcus Aurelius

You need to have the option to manage life's difficulties. Since you need to live an upbeat and happy life, this book is all about that. It is what your identity is and what you do that is important. "It is human greatness that makes an individual delightful", says Epictetus. When you create characteristics, for example, equity, serenity, mental fortitude, self-control, benevolence, or tolerance, you will become content and happy. It is not possible for anyone to swindle themselves to genuine excellence. Great and terrible lie in our decisions. It is what we decide to do with the given opportunities is important.

Joy originates from your decisions, from your intentionally picked activities. Benevolent activities will bring significant serenity. It is your most obvious opportunity for satisfaction. Do great since it is the correct activity. Try not to search for anything consequently. Do it for yourself. So, you can be the individual you need to be. Try not to be the person who yells from the housetops when done a simple demonstration.

"Essentially proceed onward to the following deed simply like the plant delivers another pack of grapes in the correct season." Marcus reminds us to do useful step for the good of our own. It is our temperament. It is our work. It is puerile conduct to determine what great you have done. As we get mature, we comprehend that making the best decision and helping other people is essentially what we need to do. It is our obligation as savvy and mindful individuals.

Do what nature requests of you. Get right to it if that is in your capacity. Try not to glance around to check whether people will think about it or not. Marcus unquestionably had more force than we have, and his activities had a greater effect than yours and mine. However, even the most influential man on earth around then reminded himself to "be happy with even the slightest advance forward and view the result as a little thing." Let's step forward at whatever point conceivable. What originates from it? It does not make a difference. "What is your calling? Being a decent man." That is the most straightforward set of working responsibilities there is. Which does not mean it is simple. Yet, when we make it our objective, we can achieve it.

Conclusion

Experiencing Stoicism is simple. Understanding and stating precisely what it actually is, however, is the precarious part. Perceiving and seeing precisely how it is applicable today and supporting you is the tricky part. Ultimately getting a handle on it and incorporating it is the aspiring part. What Stoics instructed and rehearsed in the time of combatants battling for lives and Romans associating in steaming showers is still amazingly pertinent in the period of this digital world. The shrewdness of this old way of thinking is ageless, and its incentive in the journey for a joyful and significant life is certain.

With this practical book, you have grasped the fortune map. It acquaints you with the main thinkers. It provides you a straightforward review of the way of thinking. It shows you the midpoint standards. It furnishes you with amazing Stoic Practices to apply in your difficult life.

Furthermore, it tells you the best way to interpret it from the book to activity in reality. Many people find it difficult to confront their apprehensions and battles. They do not know what to do about their burdensome sentiments. How to manage the demise of their companion? How to deal with their outrage? How to become surer?

We are as much in need of a way of thinking that shows us how to live as we were. Stoicism encourages you to live and carry on an incredible life. Whatever you are experiencing, there is a recommendation from the Stoics that can help. Notwithstanding the way of thinking's age, its astuteness regularly feels shockingly present-day and new. It can assist you with building endurance and quality for your difficult life. It can assist you with getting sincerely versatile, so you will neither get irked around by outside functions nor will others have the option to press your catches. It can train you to deal with yourself and remain quiet amidst a storm. It can assist you with settling on choices and, in this manner, definitely streamline ordinary living.

Practicing Stoicism encourages you to grow as a person. It instructs you to carefully live by many attractive qualities, such as mental fortitude, tolerance, self-control, quietness, constancy, pardoning, thoughtfulness, and modesty. Its numerous anchors offer security and direction and will step up your certainty. You can get that as well. The Stoic way of thinking makes an easy path of life, a reachable objective for everyone, regardless of whether you are rich or poor, solid or wiped out, knowledgeable or not. It has no effect on your capacity to enjoy a quality lifestyle. The Stoics were living evidence that it is workable for somebody to be ousted to a remote location and still be more joyful than somebody living in a royal residence.

They saw very well that there is just a free association between outside conditions and happiness. In Stoicism, how you manage the given circumstances matters substantially more. Stoics perceived that it relies upon the development of one's character, on one's decisions and activities instead of what occurs in the wild world around us. We are liable for our own thriving. We are liable for not letting our joy rely upon outside conditions — we should not let the downpour, irritating outsiders, or a spilling clothes washer choose our prosperity. Else, we become powerless casualties of life conditions wild.

As a Stoic, you discover that no one but you can demolish your life, and no one but you can decline to leave your internal identity alone vanquished by whatever terrible test life tosses at you. Thus, Stoicism encourages us to live by many qualities that add to enthusiastic versatility, quiet certainty, and a reasonable heading throughout everyday life. Much the same as an old dependable strolling stick, it is a manual forever dependent on the reason as opposed to confidence, a guide that underpins us in the quest for self-authority, tirelessness, and astuteness. Emotionlessness improves us and shows us how to dominate throughout everyday life. Its incredible mental methods are practically indistinguishable from those presently demonstrated to be powerful by research in the logical investigation called Positive Psychology.

If you buckle down, you will see fruitful results, and once you are effective, you will be content and happy at that point. Many people do not get joyful. They do not improve at all. They thoughtlessly walk around life lacking clear bearing, consistently commit similar errors, and would not be any more like a happy life. It should be an easy decision for many of us to receive a way of thinking of life that offers direction, bearing, and a bigger significance to life. Without that compass, there is a danger that regardless of all our benevolent activities, we will go around aimlessly, pursue useless things, and wind up carrying on with an unfulfilling life brimming with enthusiastic affliction, second thoughts, and dissatisfaction.

Give Stoicism a chance to manage the theory of life. There is nothing to lose and a lot to pick up. The guarantee of this book is the guarantee of the Stoic way of thinking. It teaches you how to live a remarkably glad and easily streaming life and how to hold that even notwithstanding affliction. It prepares you for anything, similar to a pinnacle of solidarity—steady, profoundly established, genuinely strong, and shockingly quiet and careful even amidst an inferno.

Stoicism shows you the path as well as gives you the way to an easy path. You should walk the way, turn the key, and enter.

In this way Life is all about the present time. The time has come to begin your preparation. Preparing in Stoicism is somewhat similar to surfing—little hypothesis and heaps of training. At the present time, you can hardly wait to begin, and you envision yourself remaining on surfboard that is hitting waves, having a great time. Since in your first surf exercise, you get the chance to become familiar with some hypothetical parts of surfing as well. On the dry land, you practice how to paddle, spring up, and remain on the board. As such, the initial segment feels irritating—you needed to surf. You did not pursue that dry hypothesis exercise.

Shockingly rapidly, you endure the hypothesis part, and you get the opportunity to enter water, and start your training. In water, you rapidly understand that it is not all that simple, and the hypothesis part was really fundamental. It is equivalent to Stoicism. You will get the chance to hit the waves; however, you need to hit them effectively and not surrender after the initial not (many) plunges.

This book has been sorted out to present the old astuteness in an open, absorbable, and profoundly practical way. In the initial segment, you will find out about the guarantee of the way of thinking, its set of experiences, primary rationalists, and the center standards introduced as Stoic Happiness Triangle. Follow that triangle, and you are ready to disclose the way of thinking to a four-year-old.

The subsequent part is tied in with hitting the waves. It is packed with common sense guidance and activities for ordinary living. The definitive point of this immediate and clear way to deal with Stoicism is to assist you with carrying on with a happy life. We would all be able to turn into somewhat savvier and more joyful by rehearsing this superb way of thinking. It is an ideal opportunity to take a plunge into Stoicism.

www.ingramcontent.com/pod-product-compliance
Lightning Source LLC
Chambersburg PA
CBHW080458240426
43673CB00005B/226